PROOFREADING SYMBOLS

⌒	CLOSE UP SPACE (Symbol used within the line: wo⌒rd.)
✎	DELETE
∧	INSERT MISSING MATERIAL (Symbol used within the line: th∧t.)
¶	PARAGRAPH
⊙	PERIOD
∿ or *tr*	TRANSPOSE (Symbol used within the line: the/to boy.)
?	UNCLEAR

GUIDE TO RAPID REVISION

GUIDE TO
RAPID
REVISION

FOURTH EDITION

Daniel D. Pearlman
Paula R. Pearlman

Fourth Edition Prepared by
Daniel D. Pearlman
UNIVERSITY OF RHODE ISLAND

MACMILLAN PUBLISHING COMPANY
NEW YORK

COLLIER MACMILLAN PUBLISHERS
LONDON

Macmillan Publishing Company
866 Third Avenue, New York, New York 10022

Collier Macmillan Canada, Inc.

LIBRARY OF CONGRESS CATALOGING-IN-PUBLICATION DATA

Pearlman, Daniel D.
    Guide to rapid revision / Daniel D. Pearlman, Paula R. Pearlman.—
4th ed. / prepared by Daniel D. Pearlman.
        p.   cm.
    ISBN 0-02-393320-8
    1. English language—Errors of usage. 2. English language—
Rhetoric. I. Pearlman, Paula R. II. Title.
PE1460.P37 1989
808'.042—dc19   88-3934
                                                          CIP

Illustrations by Vahan Shirvanian

PRINTING: 1 2 3 4 5 6 7   YEAR: 9 0 1 2 3 4 5

PREFACE

The Fourth Edition of *Guide to Rapid Revision* marks a quarter century of the text's use in classes of every description, including freshman and advanced composition, technical and business writing, creative writing, literature, and courses in every discipline that embody our national effort to foster "writing across the curriculum." Short of a student–instructor hotline, the *Guide* acts as the closest thing possible to an instructor-over-the-shoulder for any student working independently at revision. The new edition has been revised throughout, both for substance and for style. The overall emphases, however, remain the same: brevity, accessibility, and practicality.

A Review of the Major Features:

1. *Instant access to information:* An outstanding feature of the *Guide* has always been the alphabetical arrangement of its contents in accord with the correction symbols in common use throughout the country. The Contents is, therefore, identical to the table of Correction Symbols that begins on the inside front cover.

2. *Compactness:* Even the longest sections, such as "Commas" or "Variety in Sentence Patterns," take up only a few *pages* as compared to long *chapters* in the usual college English handbook. For the student, such brevity means an effective job of revision in a minimal amount of time.

3. *Focus on problem solving:* There is not a word here that does not contribute directly to revision! "Rules" and principles of grammar and rhetoric are stripped down to a functional minimum. In the belief that a well-chosen example speaks louder than a page of abstract explanation, the pedagogical emphasis is on the illuminating example, and whatever explanations are necessary are linked to concrete examples modeling the solution of specific problems.

4. *Clarity:* The style throughout is direct and to the point, neither patronizing nor condescending. The author assumes that the reader is an intelligent seeker of guidance through the brambles of written usage.

Features New to the Fourth Edition:

1. Completely rewritten are the sections "Case," "Coherence," "Paragraphing," "Transitions," "Variety in Sentence Patterns," and "Wordiness."

2. A new section deals with avoiding sexist expressions.

3. For the further convenience of users, the list of correction symbols has been expanded to include some helpful new ones and alternates.

4. A topically organized listing of all sections of the *Guide* is provided to facilitate its use as a classroom teaching text. For example, instructors interested in focusing for part of the semester on topics such as sentence correctness or punctuation will find listed under each topic the relevant sections in the *Guide.* It is hoped that instructors will be pleasantly surprised on glancing at the topical listing to note the considerable attention paid in so brief a guide to many matters involving writing style, and not only matters of basic correctness.

5. The even greater use of cross-referencing in the Fourth Edition directs the reader to information located elsewhere in the *Guide* that could deepen understanding of the specific problem at hand.

For those instructors who wish to assign a workbook, please note that the Second Edition of the *Guide to Rapid Revision Workbook* appears simultaneously with the Fourth Edition of the *Guide.* The *Workbook* offers intensive practice in the techniques of revision espoused in the *Guide* and stresses *the generation of new sentences and paragraphs,* not just the recognition and filling in of correct answers.

I am deeply grateful for the countless useful suggestions that have come from instructors and students who have used this text during its past three incarnations. With regard to much of the new material that I have been particularly pleased to incorporate into this Fourth Edition, I am most indebted to the sharp eyes and even sharper wits of John R. Deitrick of Beckner Junior College and Kathleen Black of Northwestern College. I'd also like to thank Margaret L. Allison, Mesa Community College; Lucile M. Morse, East Central University; Lois H. Westerlund, Roger Williams College; John O'Connor, George Mason University; Robert Jones, Oregon State University; and Gary D. Christenson, Elgin Community College for their helpful comments on various drafts of the manuscript.

I appreciate all unsolicited comments concerning the improvement of the *Guide*, and I reply to them personally. The present text embodies every helpful criticism offered that did not ask for major changes in the book's scope and purpose.

D. D. P.

TO THE INSTRUCTOR

I have long felt that the process of revision, central in the development of writing skills, has not been given the full attention it merits among books published for courses in English composition. Most composition handbooks follow a sequential and topical plan designed for *study* of the problems of writing but not necessarily for their immediate solution. Students who turn to these texts for help when revising papers that the instructor has marginally annotated find that they lose time hunting for the passages relevant to their particular problem. In fact, they must often read as much as a full chapter for each error they have made.

The present *Guide*, planned entirely with the realities of revision in mind, gives students *immediate* answers to specific problems, offers sufficient information to solve them, and yet does so with *brevity*. Using the book independently, students may feel as if an instructor were personally going over their papers with them point by point in conference.

Among the major time-saving features of this *Guide* are its compactness and the alphabetical arrangement of its contents. Another convenience is a table of correction symbols that begins on the inside front cover. The table presents the most common symbols used by English instructors throughout the country, and on the inside back cover there is space for students to list extra symbols that you may use from time to time. In the text are many realistic examples, often culled from actual student papers, of various types of writing deficiency. Many of these examples are followed by brief explanations that show exactly how to apply the general rule for revision.

Because the *Guide* is designed for independent use by

students, you could have your classes spend a period now and then revising their papers, *Guide* in hand, under your direct supervision. The clear, compact treatment of each topic in this *Guide* should enable students to overcome a number of their weaknesses in short order; meanwhile, demands on you for individual help will be reduced to a workable minimum. You may find, also, that if students are required to maintain the progress charts included at the end of this *Guide*, you will be able to diagnose at a glance, during conferences, their overall writing problems.

Guide to Rapid Revision is valuable both in courses where a traditional handbook of composition is assigned and in those, also, where no such handbook is used. The *Guide* substitutes for the larger handbooks because it contains an adequate treatment, despite its small physical compass, of the basics of English style, usage, and mechanics.

TOPICAL CONTENTS

Instructors who would benefit from a handbook-style *topical* approach to the concepts covered in this guide will find helpful the following logical groupings (with some inevitable overlap) of related sections:

WRITING STYLE

Abstract Expressions	Mixed Construction	Split Infinitive
Ambiguity	Paragraph	Subordination
Awkward	Parallelism	Transitions
Choppy Sentences	Passive Voice	Triteness
Coherence	Pronoun Reference	Vagueness
Diction	Repetition	Variety in Sentence
Emphasis	Sexist Expressions	Patterns
Logic	Shift in Point	Wordiness
	of View	

SENTENCE CORRECTNESS

Agreement	Comma Splice	Incomplete
Coherence	Dangling Modifier	Construction
Comparison	Fragmentary	Misplaced Modifier
	Sentence	

Mixed Construction	Pronoun Reference	Shift in Point
Parallelism	Run-On Sentence	of View
		Subordination

PUNCTUATION

Apostrophe	Dash	Parentheses
Brackets	Ellipsis	Possessive Case
Comma	Exclamation Point	Quotation Marks
Colon	Fragmentary	Run-On Sentence
Comma Splice	Sentence	Semicolon
	Hyphen	

POINTS OF GRAMMAR AND MECHANICS

Abbreviations	Case	Italics
Adjective	Capitalization	Numbers
Adverb	Comparison	Split Infinitive
Agreement	Diction	Tense
Apostrophe	Incomplete	
	Construction	

TO THE STUDENT

This book is designed to save you many hours in revising your compositions. Its explanations of English usage are brief, clear, and to the point, and it includes realistic examples that you can use in correcting your specific shortcomings. Years of teaching experience have convinced me that most of your writing problems can be eliminated in short order. In keeping the book short, I have tried to omit no information that could cast real light on your writing difficulties. Each time you revise, you learn the principles of English usage, so that you need not repeat the same mistakes.

HOW TO USE THIS GUIDE

If your instructor uses correction symbols, and you are not certain of their meaning, the alphabetically arranged table of correction symbols found at the beginning of this book will tell you what the symbols mean and what page to turn to for help. This book avoids lengthy grammatical explanations of your writing problems. Specific examples—combined with short, concrete explanations—show you how to overcome your weak points. Extensive cross-referencing, such as the advice in the "Paragraph" section to "see *Coherence* and *Transitions*," enables you to find further information related to some special aspect of the problem at hand. Pursue such cross-references if you have time. Assume, however, that the *essential* information you need is already provided in the section you are reading.

Special spelling problems are handled in the sections on abbreviations and numbers and in the Glossary of Common Errors in the "Diction" section. Otherwise, for the usual misspelled word refer to your dictionary. If you keep up to date your general Progress Chart and your Spelling Progress Chart at the end of the *Guide,* you will have an excellent understanding of your writing and spelling problems and will see what to bear down on as the term progresses.

You will find this *Guide* a valuable reference for your formal writing and revision needs. *Formal* writing is more conservative in grammar and phrasing than *informal* writing. The emphasis in formal writing is on the objective, impersonal communication of ideas and information, whereas informal writing tends to focus on self-expression and highlights the writer's own personality. Almost all the writing you will be asked to do in school, or in the business and professional world, is of the formal sort.

CONTENTS

ABBREVIATIONS ——————— ab

Spell out words in full and do not use telegraphic prose.

As a general rule, do not use abbreviations in formal writing. Some common abbreviations to avoid in your writing are *&*, *gov't.*, *U.S.*, *U.S.A.*, *thru.* Use *and, government, United States, United States of America, through.*

Especially avoid using *etc.*, short for *et cetera*, meaning *and so forth.* If you really want to say *and so forth*, write it out, but usually you will do better to write out the specific ideas you have in mind rather than to ask your readers to guess at what you mean.

EXCEPTIONS: With proper names, abbreviated titles are preferred: *Dr., Mr., Messrs., Ms., Mrs., Mmes., Jr., Sr., St.* (Saint), *Prof.*

Standard abbreviations such as *A.M.*, *P.M.*, *A.D.*, *B.C.* and those of certain well-known organizations and government agencies such as *EPA, FBI, NATO, NASA* are also acceptable. When citing a less well-known organization, give the full name of the organization at first mention; then use its abbreviation thereafter.

Avoid the telegraphic style that results from the use of the slash [/] or parentheses [()] to connect closely related items by writers too impatient to express their ideas in a clear, logical sequence.

ABUSE OF SLASH: Our present administrative policy/program is now bankrupt.

ABUSE OF PARENTHESES: Our present administrative policy (program) is now bankrupt. (See **Parentheses**.)

BETTER: Our present administrative policy *and resulting* program are now bankrupt. [Usually the telegraphic method leaves out the important logical connection between terms that are so hastily joined together.]

NOTE: For *and/or* see the Glossary under **Diction**.

abst —— ABSTRACT EXPRESSIONS

1. Add a word or phrase to the abstract term to make it more specific.

2. Replace the abstract term with a word or explanatory passage that is more specific. (See *Vagueness*.)

1. ABSTRACT TERMS

Abstract words and phrases, like *beauty, evil,* and *progress,* have meanings that are somewhat different for each reader. Perhaps you are certain of what you mean by *progress* in a statement such as this: "America has made great progress in the last fifty years." But your reader does not know what you mean until you use a more *specific* expression such as *technological progress* or *moral progress*.

To avoid vagueness, you would no doubt need to explain an expression like *moral progress* even further. Do you mean that there are fewer murders? Do you mean that young people are more *moral*?

The effect of explaining yourself further is to get more and more *specific* and *concrete* in presenting your ideas. The more precisely you define your ideas, the less you risk being misunderstood.

2. CONCRETE TERMS

A *concrete* word refers to an actual object whose nature is generally known. For example, we all know what *tree* stands for. However, when the tree you are writing about plays an important role in your composition, it is better to use an even more specific concrete expression, like *elm* or *oak*. It is like zooming in for a close-up in movie-making:

> ABSTRACT: Politics unfairly determined the results of the recent election. [Many of us, in attempting to explain the ills of society, take the intellectually lazy way out by shrugging our shoulders and blaming everything on politics.]
>
> REVISION: A last-minute public smear campaign together with private blackmail unfairly determined the results of the recent election. [It turns out that the abstract *politics* was screening some rather interesting concrete realities.]

ADJECTIVE ———————— adj

1. **Change the marked word to an adjective.**
2. **Change the marked adjective to the proper form.**

(See *Comparison*.)

1. PREDICATE ADJECTIVES

An adjective modifies (describes) a noun or pronoun. Usually, an adjective occurs right next to the word it modifies: the *delicious* coffee. But sometimes the adjective is separated from the word it modifies by a verb, called a linking verb: The coffee smells *delicious*. The adjective *delicious* modifies the noun *coffee*. Adjectives that come after a linking verb are called *predicate adjectives*.

One common writing error that students make is placing an adverb—instead of an adjective—after a linking verb: The coffee smells *deliciously*. The most common linking verbs are all forms of *to be*, such as *is*, *are*, *was*, and the following verbs of the five senses: *sound, smell, look, feel, taste*. Use an adjective after these verbs.

WRONG: Her makeup looked *well* on her.
RIGHT: Her makeup looked *good* on her.

WRONG: The wounded animal's wail sounded *horribly* in the night.
RIGHT: The wounded animal's wail sounded *horrible* in the night.

WRONG: My roommate felt *badly* about his recent grades.
RIGHT: My roommate felt *bad* about his recent grades.

Feel (Look) Good Versus Feel (Look) Well

Ordinarily, *well* is an adverb. Use *well* as an adjective—after *feel, look*, and so on—only when you mean the opposite of *ill*. It is no compliment to tell a friend that she looks *well* today unless she has just recovered from an illness. If you simply mean that you admire her clothing or makeup, tell her that she looks *good*.

2. CORRECT FORMS OF ADJECTIVES

1. *Comparative Degree:* The comparative degree of an adjective is used when you compare two things. The com-

parative is usually formed by adding -er to adjectives of one syllable (great*er*, proud*er*) and by placing the word *more* in front of adjectives of more than one syllable (*more* useful, *more* salable). Exception: Two-syllable adjectives ending in -*y* may also add -*er*: *lazier* or *more lazy*, *angrier or more angry, lovelier* or *more lovely*.

NOTE: Do not form the comparative twice:

WRONG: Allen is a far *more better* student than Ted.
RIGHT: Allen is a far *better* student than Ted.

2. *Superlative Degree:* The superlative degree of an adjective is used when you compare more than two things. Form the superlative by adding -*est* to the end of a one-syllable adjective (great*est*, proud*est*) and by placing the word *most* in front of adjectives of more than one syllable (*most* beautiful, *most* useful). Exception: For two-syllable adjectives ending in -*y*, you may also add -*est*: For example, *laziest* or *most lazy*.

3. *Irregular Forms:* The comparative and superlative forms of some adjectives are irregular. *Good* becomes *better* (comparative) and *best* (superlative); *bad* becomes *worse* and *worst*. The following examples illustrate the point:

NOTE: Do not use the superlative in place of the comparative:

WRONG: Mary is the *best* of the two writers.
RIGHT: Mary is the *better* of the two writers. (Use *better*, not *best*, if only two individuals are being compared.)

FEWER, LESS: Look these up in the Glossary under **Diction.**

Change the marked word to an adverb – usually by adding -*ly.*

Adverbs are words that modify (describe) verbs, adjectives, or other adverbs. Most adverbs, although far from all, are made up of adjectives with -*ly* endings. Adverbs limit the meanings of the words they modify by setting specific conditions such as *how* (*unusually* lucky), *when* (left *immediately*), and *where* (far *ahead*).

Certain verbs like *sing, dance,* and *write* often mislead people into using an adjective where an adverb is needed:

WRONG: He sang *beautiful.* [His song may have been beautiful, but we want to describe his action.]
RIGHT: He sang *beautifully.*

NOTE: Not all adverbs end in -*ly.* Some common adverbs have unusual forms—*well, rather, very, late, soon, seldom, often, now, later, today, tomorrow*—and some prepositions double as adverbs: He turned *around*, fell *behind*, jumped *up.* The adverbs *well* and *very* are often used incorrectly in favor of adjectives:

WRONG: She writes *good.*
RIGHT: She writes *well.* [The adverb *well* specifies *how* she writes.]

WRONG: They had a *real* good time.
RIGHT: They had a *very* good time. [In careless or casual speech you often hear *real* misused as an adverb, as in *a real nice day.* A better correction than *very* nice might be a single expressive word like *wonderful.* See **Triteness.**]

AGREEMENT ――――――――― agr

1. **Make the verb in this sentence agree in number with its subject. If the verb is in the singular, change it to the plural, and vice versa.**
2. **Make the pronoun in this sentence agree in number with its antecedent – the word the pronoun refers to.**

1. SUBJECT–VERB AGREEMENT

In the present tense, all verbs are the same in both the singular and the plural—except for the *third-person singular,* where an *-s* is added. The third-person pronouns are *he, she,* and *it:* He moves; she moves; it moves. Most of the time you will be using words that can be replaced by *he, she,* or *it: John* moves; *Barbara* moves; *the cloud* moves. Still, the verb ends in *-s.*

All other pronouns, singular or plural, agree with the verb without the *-s:* I *work;* we *work;* you *work.* Plural words that can be replaced by the pronoun *they* also agree with the verb without the *-s:* The *machines* work.

In simple sentences you can easily see how all third-person singular subjects take or agree with *-s* verbs and how all other subjects take the form without *-s:*

- *He* always *speaks* so carefully.
- Our *refrigerator makes* clanking noises. [*Refrigerator* can be replaced by *it.*]
- *They live* right under a volcano.
- *Carol, Iris,* and *John live* very comfortably. [*Carol, Iris, and John* can be replaced by *they.*]

You are likely to make mistakes in sentences when you are not sure what the subject is or when you do not know whether the subject is third-person singular or plural.

Do not be derailed by words and phrases that come

7

between the subject and verb. Find the *simple* subject (the subject stripped of all its modifying words and phrases). *The simple subject is never part of a prepositional phrase.* But prepositional phrases often follow the subject and might confuse you, as in the following sentences:

WRONG: The solution to all our problems *are* staring us in the face.

RIGHT: The solution to all our problems *is* staring us in the face. [The subject is *solution,* not *problems;* the words *to all our problems* constitute a prepositional phrase. You can find the simple subject if you block off, temporarily, all prepositional phrases in the sentence.]

NOTE: For the present tense of the verb *to be,* all third-person singular subjects agree with the verb form *is.* All other subjects agree with *are*—except, of course, for the *first*-person singular *I am.*

WRONG: One of the requirements of membership *are* monthly dues payments.

RIGHT: One of the requirements of membership *is* monthly dues payments. [Notice that two prepositional phrases, *of the requirements* and *of membership,* come between the subject *one* and the verb.]

In some cases, normal sentence order is reversed and the subject *follows* the verb:

WRONG: After the cheerleaders *come* the band.

RIGHT: After the cheerleaders *comes* the band. [The *band* comes!]

WRONG: There *is* two dogs in the park.

RIGHT: There *are* two dogs in the park.

Be careful of sentences beginning with *there* followed immediately by a verb. *There* will not be the subject. The subject will always follow the verb. In the above example, because *two dogs* is a plural subject, it takes the verb *are.*

When singular subjects are joined by *either . . . or* or

neither . . . nor, use the singular verb. Remember that singular subjects are ones that can be replaced by *he, she,* or *it;* singular verbs usually end in *-s:*

> WRONG: Neither the captain nor the coach *try* very hard to win.
> RIGHT: Neither the captain nor the coach *tries* very hard to win.

If one of the subjects joined by *either . . . or* or *neither . . . nor* is not singular, then the verb agrees with the nearer subject:

> WRONG: Neither the captain nor the coaches *tries* very hard to win.
> RIGHT: Neither the captain nor the coaches *try* very hard to win. [*Coaches,* a *they* word, is nearer to the verb.]

> WRONG: Neither the coaches nor the captain *try* very hard to win.
> RIGHT: Neither the coaches nor the captain *tries* very hard to win. [The third-person singular, *captain,* is nearer to the verb; *captain* takes the singular *-s* form.]

2. PRONOUN—ANTECEDENT AGREEMENT

When the antecedent—the word that a pronoun refers to—is singular, use a singular pronoun. When the antecedent is plural, use a plural pronoun:

> RIGHT: *Sandra* knows *she* is smart. [The pronoun *she* refers to *Sandra. Sandra* is the antecedent, the word that the pronoun *she* refers to.]
> RIGHT: A short time after buying her *books,* she somehow lost *them.* [The antecedent of *them* is *books.*]

Notice that in both these examples, the pronoun agrees in number with its antecedent: *She* is singular, as is *Sandra; them* is plural, as is *books.*

> WRONG: Vacations offer us opportunities for self-renewal, but *it is* often wasted when we fail to plan ahead for *it.*

RIGHT: Vacations offer us opportunities for self-renewal, but *they are* often wasted when we fail to plan ahead for *them*. [*Vacations*, a plural, is the antecedent of *they*. The correction not only changes *it* to *they*, but changes the verb of the first *it* from *is* to *are*.]

WRONG: I like to read a book now and then just for my own pleasure, especially if *they are* short and topical.
RIGHT: I like to read a book now and then just for my own pleasure, especially if *it* is short and topical.

Writers and speakers face the problem of which pronoun to use when antecedents such as *each, everybody, everyone, anybody, nobody, no one, one, either, neither* are singular. In the past, the solution has been to use the third-person-singular masculine pronoun:

- Everyone in the class raised *his* hand.

However, this solution leaves out women. Several ways out of this dilemma are briefly illustrated under **Sexist Expressions**, 1.

amb ———————— AMBIGUITY

Revise the ambiguous passage to make it clearly mean one thing only. Ambiguity means *double* meaning or *vagueness* of meaning:

AMBIGUOUS: This morning our bus was *held up* by a pair of red-jacketed men at a construction site. [Was this a *hold-up* in the criminal sense?]
CLEAR: This morning our bus was *detained* by a pair of red-jacketed men at a construction site.

AMBIGUOUS: Bob asked Jack if Iris liked *him*.
CLEAR: "Does Iris like you?" Bob asked Jack. [The use of a direct quotation will show whether *him* means Bob or Jack.]

AMBIGUOUS: Visitors sometimes leave sessions with the President *feeling frustrated and even a bit alarmed.* [This sentence, quoted from a news story, may leave *us* feeling frustrated too! After all, who is feeling frustrated, the visitors or the President? As it stands, there are two possible answers, each shown in the clearly revised versions that follow:]

CLEAR 1: After leaving sessions with the President, visitors sometimes feel frustrated and even a bit alarmed.

CLEAR 2: After visitors leave sessions with the President, he sometimes feels frustrated and even a bit alarmed.

(See **Misplaced Modifier**, **Pronoun Reference**, and **Vagueness**.)

APOSTROPHE ——————— ap, apos

Add a missing apostrophe, or remove one you have mistakenly used. The apostrophe has three main uses:

1. It marks the possessive case of nouns.
2. It indicates a contraction.
3. It indicates plurals of letters, abbreviations, and numbers.

1. POSSESSIVE CASE OF NOUNS

For nouns, both singular and plural, that do not end in *s*, form the possessive by adding *'s*: the *bird's* nest; the *children's* party; the *person's* name.

For plural nouns that end in *s*, add the apostrophe only: the *soldiers'* uniforms (uniforms of the soldiers); the *ladies'* coats (coats for ladies).

For singular nouns that end in *s*, add *'s*. But if the last *s* would be awkward to pronounce, drop it and add only the apostrophe: the *boss's* daughter (daughter of the boss) but *Rameses'* kingdom, *Moses'* leadership.

NOTE: Do not use an apostrophe in the personal pronouns *its, his, hers, ours, theirs, whose.*

2. CONTRACTIONS

Always use the apostrophe to show the omission of a letter or letters in the contracted form of words: *wasn't* (was not), *I've* (I have), *we'll* (we will), *you're* (you are), *it's* (it is).

NOTE: As a general rule, avoid contractions in formal writing.

3. PLURALS OF LETTERS, ABBREVIATIONS, AND NUMBERS

Use the apostrophe for plurals of lowercase letters: *n's, x's, p's,* and *q's.* But for capital letters you can follow either of two styles: *Qs* or *Q's*—unless the *s* alone would be confusing, such as *As.*

Use the apostrophe for plurals of abbreviations containing periods: *B.A.'s, C.P.A.'s, R.N.'s.* But for abbreviations without periods you have a choice of two styles: *VIPs* or *VIP's.*

You have a choice of two styles for the plurals of numbers: either *5's, 10's,* the *1900's* or *5s, 10s,* the *1900s.*

NOTE: Whenever you choose a style, use it consistently throughout your composition.

awk —————————— AWKWARD

Rethink and rewrite the marked passage.

Awkward is a catchall term. It may refer to one specific problem in your writing or any combination of problems. It may point simply to an error in diction (inexact use of a word) or to a much larger problem, such as the lack of coherence in a series of sentences. A similar catchall term is *sentence structure* (SS), which may point to anything from an obvious structural error to a messy passage requiring rewriting. Upon analysis, some problems marked *awkward* can be given more specific names such as ambiguity, choppy sentences, mixed construction, faulty parallelism, repetition, wordiness. In using the term *awkward*, your instructor probably expects you to recognize what is wrong at a glance without more technical advice. If you see no problem with the passage marked *awk*, make an appointment to see your instructor as soon as possible. If on rereading the passage you find it unsatisfactory, then use your own judgment in rewriting it. Sometimes a passage contains such a severe combination of problems that your instructor simply marks it *awk* in order not to discourage you by listing them all. In rewriting, put aside what you have originally written and focus on the original *thought* you were trying to express. Rethink your ideas as well as rewrite them. Most such problems disappear if, in revising, you make a sincere effort to concentrate on the original *idea* you were after:

> AWKWARD: Due to the number of students in college, they appear to be all equal because everyone is experiences the same things.

There are several things wrong with the above sentence. Basically, the statement lacks logical coherence. In addition, the use of *due to* is an error in diction, and *is experiences* results from simple carelessness. To call this sentence *awkward* rightly points the student back to the drawing board for total rethinking and revision:

> IMPROVED: There are so many students in college undergoing the same experiences that in many ways they seem to be copies of one another.

> AWKWARD: Being an avid fan of country music and having a boyfriend who is a definite rock fan provides a look at the two different types of music.

It is hard to say specifically what is wrong here. Is *being . . . and having . . .* a double subject? If so, it is plural and does not agree with the singular verb, *provides.* But *being . . . and having . . .* sounds more like a *dangling modifier* looking for a missing subject. Since the two halves of the sentence do not fit together, the problem may be *mixed construction.* Who knows? *Awkward* is probably the best label for such an undeveloped sentence:

> IMPROVED: Being an avid fan of country music and having a boyfriend who is a definite rock fan, I get a good look at both kinds of music.

[/] ——————————— BRACKETS

Add brackets, or if you have used brackets incorrectly, change to parentheses.

1. Use brackets to set off your own explanatory comments from the body of a text that you are quoting or editing:

   "Every village, every town [in Spain] is the centre of an intense social and political life," says Brenan.

If you were to use parentheses instead of brackets around *in Spain,* your reader would think them to be Brenan's words and not yours.

2. Use brackets to avoid parentheses within parentheses:

   Kafka's most extraordinary work begins with the description of a man suddenly changed into a giant beetle (*The Metamorphosis* [Original German edition: Leipzig, 1915]).

CAPITALIZATION ——————— cap

Capitalize the word or words indicated, or change them to begin with a small letter if you have used capitals incorrectly.

1. Capitalize proper names. These are the names of specific persons, places, things, races, institutions, organizations: *Joe Fox,* the *East River, Black, Tilden High School,* the *United Nations, Indian.* The word *the* beginning names of organizations should not be capitalized: *the* United Nations, *the* Police Athletic League.
2. Capitalize the first letter of every word beginning a sentence, including the first word of every quoted sentence: *He* said proudly, "*Everything* is in order."
3. In titles of books, articles, movies, and plays, always capitalize the first and every word except short prepositions, coordinating conjunctions, and articles of four or fewer letters: *The Old Man and the Sea; Much Ado About Nothing; Life with Father.*

CASE ——————————— case

Use the correct case of a pronoun.

Many of the errors you make in *case* are carryovers of informal speech patterns into the formal situation of writing, where a high degree of grammatical accuracy is usually expected.

Case is the form a pronoun takes when performing a certain role in a sentence. Three cases exist in English: the subjective case, the objective case, and the possessive case. (For nouns in the possessive case, see **Apostrophe**.) How do you know what case to use for a particular pronoun? That depends on your ability to recognize the subjects and objects in sentences. You probably have fewest problems with the possessive case, and those are usually spelling problems.

In a simple sentence like "She hired him," we see the typical English sentence pattern: subject (*She*) + verb (*hired*) + direct object (*him*). To use case correctly, use the subjective case in positions occupied by subjects and the objective case in positions occupied by objects. Two other sentence positions occupied by objects are important to note: indirect objects and objects of prepositions. Verbs may have not only direct objects, but *indirect objects* as well: She gave *him* (*her, me, us,* . . .) a job. You can tell when *him* is an indirect object if you can "translate" it to mean *to him* or *for him*. She gave *him* a job equals She gave a job *to him*. Another position for objects is after prepositions (*to, for, of, by, with,* and so on). When the object of a preposition is a pronoun, it must be in the objective case: They voted for *him* and *me*; " . . . for *whom* the bell tolls."

Sample Sentences Analyzed for Uses of Case

- I wrote her a letter about him, asking her several important questions. (*I* [subj.] *wrote* [vb.] *her* [ind. obj.] a *letter* [dir. obj.] *about* [prep.] *him* [obj. of prep.], asking *her* [ind. obj.] several important *questions* [dir. obj.].
- I urged her to send me a reply with an extra copy for him. (*I* [subj.] *urged* [vb.] *her* [dir. obj.] *to send* [vb.] *me* [ind. obj.] a *reply* [dir. obj.] *with* [prep.] an extra *copy* [obj. of prep.] *for* [prep.] *him* [obj. of prep.]

Common Case Problems

1. *The double subject.* Do not use the objective case in double subjects:

   WRONG: *Him* and Claire rehearsed the duet.
   RIGHT: *He* and Claire rehearsed the duet. [The subjective case *he* is correct. The test for the correct case is to drop "and Claire." "Him . . . rehearsed" sounds wrong.]

2. *The double object.* Do not use the subjective case in double objects:

WRONG: Kate telephoned both Suzanne and *he.*
RIGHT: Kate telephoned both Suzanne and *him.* [*Him* is a direct object. The test for the correct case is to drop "both Suzanne and." "Telephoned . . . he" sounds wrong.]

WRONG: Bill gave her and *I* the information.
RIGHT: Bill gave her and *me* the information. [*Me* is an indirect object.]

WRONG: They returned the album to Myra and *I.*
RIGHT: They returned the album to Myra and *me.* [*Me* is the object of a preposition.]

3. *Pronoun + appositive as subject.* Use the subjective case for sentences beginning with a pronoun plus an appositive in the subject position:

WRONG: *Us* students are very practical people.
RIGHT: *We* students are very practical people. [*Students,* part of the subject of this sentence, is an *appositive,* a noun that renames or identifies the noun or pronoun before it. If you drop the appositive *students,* you can see that "Us . . . are very practical" sounds wrong.

4. *Than/as + pronoun.* Use the subjective case for comparisons ending with a pronoun intended as a subject:

WRONG: Hilary skates better than *me.*
RIGHT: Hilary skates better than *I.* [The sentence would logically continue as "Hilary skates better than *I do*" or "than *I skate.*" The subjective case–*I*–is needed because the pronoun after *than* is the subject of an elliptical–unfinished–clause: *I skate.*]

WRONG: Joan is as intelligent as *him.*
RIGHT: Joan is as intelligent as *he.* [Think: "as *he is.*" *He* is the subject of the elliptical clause *he is.*]

NOTE: If the pronoun after *than* or *as* is intended as the *object* of the omitted verb, then it should be in the objective case:

EXAMPLE: John likes him better than *me*. [Think of the sentence with the full elliptical clause included: "John likes him better than *he likes me*."]

5. *To be + subjective case.* Use the subjective case for any pronoun immediately following the verb *to be* (*am, are, is, was,* and so on):

WRONG: It was *her* who borrowed my new skis.
RIGHT: It was *she* who borrowed my new skis.

6. *Who (whoever)/whom (whomever).* In choosing between *who* (*whoever*) and *whom* (*whomever*), use *who* if the pronoun you want is the *subject* of its own clause. Use *whom* (*whomever*) if the pronoun you want is an *object* in its own clause:

EXAMPLE: *Who* gave me the flowers? [Correct. *Who* is the grammatical subject of this question.]
EXAMPLE: *Whom* are you angry with? [Correct. If you turn the sentence around, you get, "You are angry with *whom?*" and you can see that *whom* is the object of the preposition *with*.]
EXAMPLE: *Whom* the Gods would destroy they first make mad. [Correct. *Whom* is the object of the verb *destroy* in the clause "whom the Gods would destroy."]
EXAMPLE: She avoided *whoever* upset her. [Correct. You would expect the object of the verb *avoided* to be *whomever*. It is not. The object of *avoided* is the whole clause *whoever upset her*. *Whoever* is correct because it acts as the *subject* of its own clause, *whoever upset her*.]

7. *Whose/who's and its/it's.* Do not confuse certain forms of the possessive case with contractions. *Whose* and *its* imply possession or ownership:

EXAMPLE: *Whose* down parka is this?

EXAMPLE: Take the parrot out of *its* cage.

Who's and *it's* are contractions and are used informally to replace *who is, it is,* and *it has:*

EXAMPLE: *Who's* (*Who is*) the culprit responsible for this vandalism?
EXAMPLE: *It's* (*It is*) your last chance.
EXAMPLE: *It's* (*It has*) been a long day.

8.   *Pronoun + gerund:* Use the possessive case for a pronoun that occurs immediately before a gerund (an *-ing* word used as a noun):

EXAMPLE: She did not mind *my* having a second helping. [Correct. Do not write *"me* having."]
EXAMPLE: We look forward to *your* joining us. [Correct. Do not write *"you* joining."]

NOTE: For nouns in the possessive case, see **Apostrophe**.

CHOPPY SENTENCES —— choppy

Revise your series of short, choppy sentences by varying your sentence patterns. Do not simply combine your sentences with *ands* or semicolons. The result would be a series of *longer* choppy sentences known as *stringy* sentences. If you master the simple art of using a variety of sentence types, your style will become much smoother:

CHOPPY: She had a very good coat. It was with her almost everywhere. It was a dark-blue woollen coat with a blue lining. It was full length and conservative looking. At one time it had a belt, but that was later lost. On the sleeves some worn spots were starting to appear. They showed how much she used it. It kept her warm on cold nights, and that was what counted most.

SMOOTH: She had a very good coat *that* she took with her almost everywhere. Conservative looking, it was a full-length, dark-blue woollen *garment* with a blue lining. *In spite of* losing the belt, she used the coat *so much that* worn spots were starting to appear on the sleeves. *As far as she was concerned,* what counted most was that it kept her warm on cold nights.

ANALYSIS: A choppy paragraph of eight sentences is rewritten to form a much smoother paragraph of four sentences that is slightly shorter (68 words for the smoother version versus 72 for the choppy version) even though two new phrases have been added. In the revised paragraph, the italicized words and phrases do not appear in the original. For the most part, they reveal logical relationships between thoughts, relationships that are not clearly seen in the original. To revise choppy writing, do not simply combine short sentences into longer ones, but use the resources of phrasing and sentence structure *to reveal logical relationships between thoughts.* The main techniques of revision used above are discussed in detail under **Subordination**, **Transitions**, and **Variety in Sentence Patterns**.

coh ——————— COHERENCE

Completely rewrite the indicated passage. As it now stands, the material does not make clear, logical sense. The parts are not organized in a logical pattern.

Coherence literally means "holding together." Other words for coherence are *organization, order, arrangement,* and *pattern.* When your phrases, sentences, and ideas hold together, your writing has coherence. In coherent writing, the train of thought is easy to follow. Connections and relationships be-

tween ideas are clear. Major ideas stand out from minor points, and ideas of equal importance receive equal emphasis.

LOGICAL ORDER OF IDEAS: Simply throwing down your ideas as they occur to you does not guarantee coherence. The mind very often leaps ahead of the pen, so give your pen time to catch up and arrange your thoughts in a logical sequence. One idea should lead clearly to the next in an orderly, step-by-step pattern with no missing links. There should be a reason that your third sentence follows the second, not vice versa.

LINKAGE OF IDEAS: A good writer uses various devices to clarify the relationships *between* ideas. A good writer provides links or transitions that lead the reader from sentence to sentence without confusion. Consider the links—the italicized words—between the following two sentences:

21

> Jogging is a fast-growing sport. *In fact,* there is a new sports magazine on the market this month *that devotes the entire issue to jogging.*

In fact is a transition between the two sentences, a logical bridge telling the reader that factual evidence is at hand to support the first statement. The clause *that devotes the entire issue to jogging* links the two sentences by repeating the main idea of the first sentence, including the key word *jogging.* Without these two devices you would have the following *incoherent* piece of writing:

> Jogging is a fast-growing sport. There is a new sports magazine on the market this month.

There are four main ways to link ideas:

1. Transitional words or phrases.
2. Repetition of key words or ideas.
3. Pronouns.
4. Demonstrative adjectives.

1. TRANSITIONAL WORDS OR PHRASES

EXAMPLE: More than a dozen condors have bred successfully in captivity. *As a result,* the chance of their extinction seems remote. [*As a result* is a transitional phrase showing the logical connection between the two sentences. Among commonly used transitions are *for example, however, consequently, first of all, on the other hand.* See **Transitions.**]

2. REPETITION OF KEY WORDS OR IDEAS

EXAMPLE: Most economists agree that inflation is caused primarily by *declining productivity.* It is the *declining levels of productivity,* not the national debt, that threaten the economic base of our country.

EXAMPLE: The conventional stereo receiver is not capable of reducing *distortion* before it occurs. *Garbled sound* must be eliminated by manually adjusting the dial. [*Garbled sound* repeats the idea of *distortion.*]

3. PRONOUNS

EXAMPLE: Professor Donaldson gave the assignment last week. *He* emphasized that *it* would be due today. [Both *he* and *it* are pronouns that refer to nouns in the previous sentence.]

4. DEMONSTRATIVE ADJECTIVES

EXAMPLE: The jury reached a decision in less than twenty minutes. *This* verdict would affect the defendant for the next twenty years. [Demonstrative adjectives point back to previous ideas. There are four demonstrative adjectives: *this, that, these, those.*]

Passage Lacking Coherence

Some people feel that public schools have the right to ban certain books from their libraries. *Huckleberry Finn* has been banned off and on ever since its publication. *The Catcher in the Rye* is often banned. This is in other people's opinion a violation of freedom of speech.

The Above Passage Revised

(*Note:* Added linking devices are in bold print.)

Some people feel that public schools have the right to ban certain books from their libraries. **For example,** *Huckleberry Finn* has been banned off and on ever since its publication. **Another book** often banned is *The Catcher in the Rye.* **Such** a **banning of books** is in other people's opinion a violation of freedom of speech. [**For example** is a transitional phrase; **such** is a pronoun; and **banning of books** is a repetition of key words.]

Place the colon after an introductory statement to call attention to what follows, such as:

1. **An explanation.**
2. **A list of items.**
3. **A long quotation.**

> **NOTE:** Do not place a colon after the words *as* or *such as* or the forms of the verb *to be* (*is, are,* and so on). A colon can only come after a *complete clause.*

1. COLON BEFORE AN EXPLANATION

An explanatory *word* or *phrase* following a statement may be set off with either a colon or a dash. Generally, the longer the explanatory passage, the more suitable it is to introduce it with a colon:

> RIGHT: The quality of the food served there may be described in a single word: revolting!
> RIGHT: The quality of the food served there may be described in a single word—revolting!
> WRONG: The quality of the food served there may be described in a single word *as:* revolting!

If you use *as,* you do not need the colon. *As,* like the colon, points to the explanatory *revolting.* *As,* however, does not dramatically stop the flow of the sentence the way the colon or dash does.

> RIGHT: Small businesses must be protected through appropriate governmental action: the effective and thorough

enforcement of antitrust laws in order to maintain competition and prevent agreements and combinations destructive to business.

INAPPROPRIATE: Small businesses must be protected through appropriate governmental action—the effective and thorough enforcement of antitrust laws in order to maintain competition and prevent agreements and combinations destructive to business. [In a formal style, the colon is *preferred* but not absolutely *required*.]

When a full sentence follows a colon, you may capitalize the first word or not, as you please:

RIGHT: Here is our honest opinion: *We* think you are a crackpot.

RIGHT: Here is our honest opinion: *we* think you are a crackpot.

If a *quoted* sentence follows the colon, you *must* begin the sentence with a capital letter:

RIGHT: The sign was all too clear: "*Do* not swim in this area."

WRONG: The sign was all too clear: "*do* not swim in this area."

If you are quoting a passage that does *not* begin with a capital letter, do not supply one:

RIGHT: She has several choice descriptions of the speech: "*wobbling*," "waffling," and "wordy" were the mildest.

WRONG: She had several choice descriptions of the speech: "Wobbling," "waffling," and "wordy" were the mildest.

NOTE: If you use the words *the following* or *as follows,* expect to place a colon after them:

RIGHT: When I study I proceed *as follows:* First, I review the underlined passages in my textbook; then I accurately copy all technical words and write brief definitions for them.

2. COLON BEFORE A LIST OF ITEMS

Use a colon to introduce a series of items at the end of your sentence:

RIGHT: Be sure to take the following things with you on a long ocean voyage: plenty of books, a deck of cards, a chess set, and a warm blanket.

WRONG: On a long ocean voyage be sure to take *along:* plenty of books, a deck of cards, a chess set, and a warm blanket.

There is no natural pause after *along*, as there is after *voyage* in the previous example. Do not use the colon to interrupt the normal flow of the sentence:

RIGHT: On a long ocean voyage be sure to take *along* plenty of books, a deck of cards, a chess set, and a warm blanket.

WRONG: The things to take with you on a long ocean voyage *are:* plenty of books, a deck of cards, a chess set, and a warm blanket. [The colon after *are* is not needed and interrupts the flow of the sentence.]

RIGHT: The things to take with you on a long ocean voyage *are* plenty of books, a deck of cards, a chess set, and a warm blanket.

WRONG: On a long ocean voyage take along things *such as:* plenty of books, a deck of cards, a chess set, and a warm blanket. [Do not use a colon after *as* or *such as.*]

RIGHT: On a long ocean voyage take along things *such as* plenty of books, a deck of cards, a chess set, and a warm blanket. [No punctuation is needed after *such as.*]

3. COLON BEFORE A LONG QUOTATION

If you are quoting a long passage, especially one that consists of two or more sentences, introduce it with a *colon*, not with a comma:

In "An Apology for Idlers," Robert Louis Stevenson *says:* "There is a sort of dead-alive, hackneyed people about, who are scarcely conscious of living except in the exercise of some conventional occupation. Bring these fellows into the country, or set them aboard ship, and you will see how they pine for their desk or their study."

NOTE: It is incorrect to introduce this long passage with *says* followed by a *comma*.

COMMA —————————— C

1. **Insert a comma before a coordinating conjunction that connects two main clauses. *And, but, nor, for, or, so,* and *yet* are coordinating conjunctions.**
2. **Insert a comma after sentence parts that come before the main clause, especially long phrases and subordinate clauses.**
3. **Set off parenthetical (nonrestrictive) sentence parts with commas.**
4. **Insert commas between words, phrases, and clauses in a series.**
5. **Use a comma to separate coordinate adjectives.**

The following five instructions for using the comma will solve practically all your comma problems:

1. *Use the comma before coordinating conjunctions* (and, but, nor, for, or, so, *and* yet) *that join two main clauses:*

- I completely forgot about our date for last night, *and* I sincerely hope that you will try to understand.
- Stop going with other people behind my back, *or* I promise I'll never see you again.

EXCEPTION: If the main clauses are very short, you do not have to separate them with a comma:

- I never have *and* I never will.

2. *Use the comma after sentence elements that appear before the main clause, such as subordinate clauses and phrases:*

- *When he spoke to the student,* the instructor asked him whether he studied very much.
- *Shaking his head,* the student replied that his brothers kept the television set blaring day and night.
- *As a solution to the problem,* the instructor recommended the temporary removal of a few parts from the set.

EXCEPTION: Most short prepositional phrases that come before a main clause are not followed by a comma:

- *After a moment* the student admitted that television wasn't his only distraction from studying.

Certain introductory words and phrases, like *for example, in short, in fact, however,* and *consequently,* are used to form a bridge, or transition, from one sentence to another and are followed by a comma:

- *In short,* the student admitted that he simply disliked the course.

(See **Transitions**.)

NOTE: If a subordinate clause *follows* the main clause, normally you do *not* separate them with a comma:

- No fishing boats ventured out that day because the water was too rough. [No comma between *day* and the subordinate clause beginning with *because*.]

But modern usage is flexible. Read your sentence aloud. If you hear a definite *pause* between the main and subordinate clauses, you may separate them with a comma:

- We were very good friends, as everyone knew.

3. *Use commas to set off parenthetical sentence elements.*

NONRESTRICTIVE ELEMENTS: A sentence element is parenthetical, or *nonrestrictive*, if it supplies information that is not essential to the clear meaning of the sentence. In the following examples, the nonrestrictive elements are italicized:

● Modern automobiles, *which are smaller and more fuel efficient than ever,* strike me as more practical and attractive than the older gas guzzlers.
● She is, *I am sure,* a good sport.
● They are gone, *thank goodness.*

To test whether an element is parenthetical, remove it from the sentence. If the basic idea of the sentence remains the same, then the element you have removed is parenthetical and should be set off by commas. Read the above examples without the words in italics, and you will find that the ideas of the original sentences remain unchanged.

RESTRICTIVE ELEMENTS: Restrictive sentence elements are necessary to the meaning of the sentence, as in this example:

● Everyone who is hard of hearing should wear a hearing aid.

Notice that the clause *who is hard of hearing* is essential to the meaning of the sentence. If you remove it, the basic idea of the sentence is distorted. Restrictive elements are not set off from the rest of the sentence by commas.

4. *Use commas between items in a series.* A series consists of three or more elements, which may be single *words, phrases,* or *clauses* (these last three italicized words are in a series):

- The basement was *dark, damp,* and *cold.*

The formula for the series is *a, b,* and *c.* Also acceptable in formal writing is the formula *a, b* and *c,* where there is no comma between the last two items in the series: The basement was *dark, damp* and *cold.* Whichever form you choose, try to use it throughout a piece of writing.

- He stumbled *down the stairs, across the room,* and *through the doorway.* [A series of three prepositional phrases.]
- I whistled shrilly, I listened in vain, and I turned sadly away. [Three main clauses, if they are short, may be connected in a series by commas.]
- I asked them *when I could come, where I could stay,* and *what I could do.* [A series of three subordinate clauses.]

5. *Use commas between coordinate adjectives that come before a noun.* Coordinate adjectives are adjectives that stand in *equal* relation to the noun they modify:

- She is an *old, faithful* servant.
- Look at his *clear, twinkling* eyes.

The test for coordinate adjectives is to insert the word *and* between them and omit the comma. If the adjectives

are coordinate (equal in rank), you will feel no awkwardness: *clear and twinkling* eyes.

The test shows that the following examples are not coordinate adjectives: a *small living* room, a *little old* man. The last adjective in each pair is really treated as part of the noun. It would be awkward to say *a small and living room* or *a little and old man.* Where you can insert the *and,* use the comma. Where you cannot insert the *and,* omit the comma.

NOTE: For the use of commas with quotation marks, see the end of **Quotation Marks**.

COMMA SPLICE ———————— CS

Change the comma to a period or to a semicolon. Do not join, or splice, two separate sentences with a comma. The comma splice, a type of run-on sentence, seriously handicaps readers by preventing them from distinguishing between the end of one thought and the beginning of the next:

COMMA SPLICE: New York is a busy industrial city, thousands of cars and trucks move through it every day.
REVISION 1:   New York is a busy industrial city. Thousands of cars and trucks move through it every day.

This first revision changes the comma splice to two sentences by changing the comma after *city* to a period and capitalizing *thousands.* You could also correct the error by changing the comma after city to a semicolon:

REVISION 2:   New York is a busy industrial *city; thousands* of cars and trucks move through it every day. [Before substituting a semicolon, be certain how to use it. See **Semicolon.**]

NOTE: To avoid splicing two separate sentences with a comma, learn to recognize what makes up a separate *sentence.* At the heart of a sentence are a *subject* and a *verb.* (In the example just given, *New York* is the subject of the first sentence, and *is* is its verb.) To test further for a sentence, say your group of words out loud. If it *sounds like a complete statement* (*and* has a subject and a verb), it is likely to be a *sentence.*

A second type of comma splice occurs in sentences beginning with words such as *therefore, however, then, nevertheless, moreover, also, still, thus,* or with expressions such as *in fact, for example, that is, on the other hand, in other words.* These are transitional words or phrases that begin a new main clause or a new sentence. Most often the main clause beginning with such an expression should be linked with the previous main clause by a semicolon:

COMMA SPLICE: We packed all our luggage, then we were on our way to the airport.
REVISION: We packed all our luggage; then we were on our way to the airport. [Changing the comma after *luggage* to a semicolon removes the comma splice.]

COMMA SPLICE: She did not arrive in time, therefore, we had no choice but to leave without her. [Place a semicolon after *time.*]
REVISION: She did not arrive in time; therefore, we had no choice but to leave without her.

COMMA SPLICE: I have always loved sports, in fact, I was once the youngest member of my team in the Little League. [Place a semicolon after *sports.*]
REVISION: I have always loved sports; in fact, I was once the youngest member of my team in the Little League.

COMPARISON ———————— comp

Add the word or words needed to complete the comparison. Incomplete comparisons lead to absurd or illogical statements. (For the irregular comparative forms of *good* and *bad,* see *Adjective,* 2.)

ILLOGICAL: The traffic in New York City is worse than Chicago. [*Traffic* is illogically compared to a city!]
REVISED: The traffic in New York City is worse than *the traffic in* Chicago.
BETTER: The traffic in New York City is worse than *that* in Chicago. [Use a pronoun to avoid awkward repetition.]

ILLOGICAL: In this poem Robert Frost expresses ideas different from most other poets. [*Ideas* are illogically compared to *poets.*]
REVISED: In this poem Robert Frost expresses ideas different from *those of* most other poets.

INCOMPLETE: The auditor's income was at least as high, if not higher than, the company president's. [The complete phrase should be *as high as.*]
REVISED: The auditor's income was as high *as,* if not higher than, the company president's.

DANGLING MODIFIER ——— dang

1. **Change the dangling element into a subordinate clause by adding a subject and verb.**
2. **Change the main clause so that the subject is correctly modified by the dangling modifier.**

The modifier in your sentence *dangles* because it does not clearly and logically relate to another word in the sentence. Use either one of the above changes to revise the sentence:

DANGLING: *When sitting,* my shoulders tend to slump back. [*I*, the logical subject of the modifier, does not appear in the sentence. As now written, the sentence says *my shoulders* are sitting.]
REVISION 1: *When I sit,* my shoulders tend to slump back. [This revision changes the dangling element into a subordinate clause.]
REVISION 2: When sitting, *I* find that my shoulders tend to slump back. [This revision makes the subject of the main clause, *I*, agree with the dangling element.]

DANGLING: *To type well,* your legs must be in the correct position. [Are *your legs* doing the typing?]
REVISION 1: *If you want to type well,* your legs must be in the correct position.
REVISION 2: To type well, *you must keep* your legs in the correct position.

DANGLING: *Going home,* it started to drizzle. [Where is the subject who is *going?*]
REVISION 1: *As I was going home,* it started to drizzle.
REVISION 2: Going home, *I felt it starting* to drizzle.

DANGLING: *At the age of three,* my mother discovered I had a speech impediment. [Was mother *really* three when she discovered this?]
REVISION: *When I was three,* my mother discovered I had a speech impediment. [In this case, there is simply no *smooth* way of revising that keeps the dangling phrase *At the age of three* unchanged.]

DASH ———————————— dash

Insert or delete a *dash.*

For the most part, avoid using the dash if commas or parentheses will serve equally well. Use the dash to mark an abrupt shift in thought or to emphasize a parenthetical element. However, relying on the dash too frequently for emphasis becomes monotonous. (See **Emphasis**.)

Examples of the proper use of the dash:

- "I would like—no, as a matter of fact, I wouldn't." [Abrupt shift in thought.]
- I must admit—since you force me to tell you—that my opinion of you is not very high. [Dashes set off a parenthetical element emphatically. Parentheses muffle and make unemphatic the material they enclose.]

NOTE: Most typewriters are equipped with only a hyphen and not a dash. To type the dash, use two strokes of the hyphen key [--]. Leave no space before or after the dash.

(See **Colon**, 1.)

D ——————————— DICTION

Change the word or phrase you have used to one that is more exact in *meaning*, to one that is less *wordy*, or to one that is more suited in *tone* to the rest of your essay.

Certain errors in diction (word choice) recur frequently. Check to see if your error is dealt with in the Glossary of Common Errors in Diction that follows this section. In any case, the following suggestions are a guide for correcting and avoiding mistakes in diction:

1. Check the exact meaning of the word you have used in a large (at least desk-size) modern dictionary. You may find in some cases that your problem is spelling, as, for example, confusing *accept* with *except*. This and other common spelling errors are treated in the Glossary.
2. See a sample list of common wordy expressions under **Wordiness**.
3. Sometimes the word you choose does not fit the *tone* of the rest of your essay. Tone is the attitude the writer takes toward the subject. The tone may be solemn, humorous, conciliatory, angry, informal, technical. It may reflect any emotional or intellectual attitude imaginable.

Good dictionaries give a variety of labels to words. Check your dictionary to see whether the word you have used is labeled as slang, regional, technical, informal, or nonstandard. Nonstandard words are out of place in the formal style of standard written English that is generally expected of you.

If the particular usage of a word is *standard* (generally acceptable in cultivated speaking and writing), it will not be labeled. Some words may have different labels for different meanings: For example, a word like *cool* could have one definition with a standard meaning and another definition with a slang application.

1. GLOSSARY OF COMMON ERRORS IN DICTION

A, an. *A* is used before words that start with a consonant sound. *An* is used before words that start with a vowel sound. It is the sound, not the first *letter* of a word, that tells you to use *a* or *an*. For example, you write *an hour* because the *h* is silent and *hour* really begins with a vowel sound. On the other hand, you write *a once-in-a-lifetime chance* because *once* begins with a consonant sound (*w*), and you write *a union* because *union* begins with a consonant sound (*y*).

Accept, except. *Accept* means *to receive* or *to agree to* something: "I *accepted* his offer." *Except,* used as a verb, can only mean *to exclude:* "He was *excepted* from the list of prize winners."

Affect, effect. As a verb, *affect* means *to influence:* "Her speech *affected* many people." *To effect* as a verb means *to bring about* or *to cause:* "It is hard to *effect* a change in society." As a noun, *affect* is a technical term for *feeling.* *Effect* means *result:* "The *effect* of the blow was to split the stone in half."

Aggravate. *Aggravate* means *to make worse.* It is not a synonym for *irritate* or *annoy.* Do not write: "His snide remarks *aggravated* me." Write: "His snide remarks *irritated* me." Further insults would, of course, *aggravate* your irritation.

Allusion, illusion. An *allusion* is an indirect reference, but an *illusion* is a false or deceptive notion.

Alot, a lot. *Alot* is simply a misspelling of *a lot.* In formal writing, however, it is usually better to use *many, much,* or *very much* instead of *a lot.*

Alright. In formal English, this is an unacceptable spelling of *all right*.

Among, between. Ordinarily, *between* is used when only two items are spoken of: "I divided the food *between* the cat and the dog." *Among* relates to more than two items: "The prize money was divided *among* the three winners."

Amount, number. When things or people can be counted individually, use *number*: "I saw a large *number* of students in the hall." When you are referring to a quantity of something that is not thought of as individual, countable units, use *amount*: "A large *amount* of gold was discovered in the mountain."

And/or. Use this compound sparingly and only in a highly technical or legalistic context.

Anyways, anywheres. Use the standard forms *anyway* and *anywhere*.

Around. Do not use the colloquial *around* in expressions like "He left *around* ten o'clock." "I can recite *around* fifteen poems." Use *about*: "He left *about* ten o'clock." "I can recite *about* fifteen poems."

As. *As* in the sense of *because* is often not as clear as *because*, *for*, or *since*. "I would like to leave *because* [not *as*] I'm tired." (See *Like*.)

At. (See *Where at*.)

Awhile, a while. After a preposition, spell as two words: "I slept for a *while*." Otherwise spell as one word: "I slept *awhile*."

Because. (See *Reason is because*.)

Because of the fact that. The phrase *because of the fact that* is unnecessarily wordy. Simply use *because*.

Being as, being that. *Because* or *since* are preferred in standard English.

Beside, besides. *Beside* means *at the side of; besides* means *in addition to*. "*Besides* chicken, we ate roast beef and bananas as we sat *beside* the stream."

Bust, busted. These are slang forms of the verb *burst*. Use *burst* in present and past tenses. *Bursted* is nonstandard.

Compare to, compare with. *To compare to* means to find resemblances in things that are otherwise quite different: "He compared the coffee *to* mud." *To compare with* means to find similarities and differences between two things that are of the same sort: "He compared the female students *with* the male students and found the females brighter."

Complected. Use *complexioned. Complected* is nonstandard for *complexioned.*

Could of. This term is illiterate for *could have,* which in speech is often contracted to *could've* and misspelled *could of.* [As a general rule, avoid contractions in formal writing.]

Data. This word is a Latin plural (singular, *datum*) and is often used in English with plural verbs and pronouns: "*These* data *are* out of date." Many people accept its use in the singular: "*This* data is no longer useful." (See *Phenomena, Strata.*)

Don't. Don't is a contraction of *do not* and should not be confused with *does not* or *doesn't.* Nonstandard: "He don't mind insults." Standard: "He *doesn't* [or *does not*] mind insults." Bear in mind that contractions are acceptable in speech but not in formal writing.

Due to. Use *due to* only to connect a *noun* construction with another *noun* construction: "*Rickets* [noun] is due to a vitamin D *deficiency* [noun]." Do *not* use it to connect nouns with main clauses: Wrong: "Due to an *accident* [noun] *the traffic was backed up for miles* [main clause]." (If you are uncertain, use *because of* or *caused by,* whichever fits.)

Due to the fact that. Avoid being windy. Use *because.*

Effect. (See *Affect, effect.*)

Enthuse. In formal English, it is better to use *to be enthusiastic.*

Equally as good. Drop the *as* and write *equally good,* or use *just as good.*

Etc. This is short for the Latin *et cetera,* meaning *and so on* or *and so forth.* Avoid *etc.:* It is often a substitute for precise and detailed thinking. (See **Abbreviations.**)

Except. (See *Accept, except.*)

Farther, further. *Farther* is often preferred to express extent in *space,* whereas *further* is preferred to express extent in *time* or *degree:* "We walked *farther* into the woods." "He went *further* in condemning him than anyone expected."

Fewer, less. When referring to separate items that can be counted, use *fewer:* "You make *fewer* mistakes now than when you started." *Less* refers to the degree or amount of something we consider as a whole and not as a series of individual items: "I have *less* money now than when I started."

Hadn't ought. *Hadn't ought* is nonstandard for *should not.* Instead of writing, "I *hadn't ought* to have gone," write, "I *should not have* gone."

Healthful, healthy. Whatever *gives* health is *healthful,* "a *healthful* climate," and whatever *has* health is *healthy,* "a *healthy* person."

Illusion. (See *Allusion, illusion.*)

In regards to. Use *in regard to.*

Irregardless. The proper form is *regardless.*

It's. A contraction of *it is* and a common misspelling of the possessive pronoun *its:* "They examined *its* [not *it's*] contents." Use *it's,* and other contractions, only in *informal* written English and in recording actual *speech.*

Kind of, sort of. *Kind of* and *sort of* are informal expressions. In formal written English, use *somewhat, rather, a little:* "She was *somewhat* [not *kind of*] annoyed."

Lay, lie. When you mean *to put,* use *lay.* The forms of *to lay* are "I *lay* the book down" (present), "I *laid* the book down" (past), and "I *have laid* the book down" (present perfect). When you mean *to recline,* use *lie.* The forms of *to lie* are "I *lie* in my bed" (present), "I *lay* in my bed" (past), and "I *have lain* in my bed" (present perfect).

Less. (See *Fewer, less.*)

Like, as, as if. *Like* is a preposition and is properly used in phrases *like* this or the following: "He looks *like* my father." It is improperly used when followed by a clause.

Misuse: "It looks *like* my father enjoys your company."
Revision: Change *like* to *as if:* "It looks *as if* my father
enjoys your company." In the sentence "I behaved *like*
I was told to," change *like* to *as,* "I behaved *as* I was
told to."

May of, might of. The terms *may of* and *might of* are illiterate
for *may have, might have.* (See *Could of.*)

Media. *Media* is the plural form of *medium;* it takes a plural
verb: "Some advertising *media are* morally harmful, and
the *medium* that sins the most in this respect *is* television." A singular verb with *media* is nonstandard. (See
Data, Phenomena, Strata.)

Mighty. Use a standard word like *very:* "I was *very* [not
mighty] tired."

Most. Use *almost:* "I saw them *almost* [not *most*] every day."

Must of. This term is illiterate for *must have.* (See *Could of.*)

Off of. Drop the *of.*

Phenomena. In formal English, *phenomena* is the plural,
phenomenon the singular.

Quite. Do not overuse *quite* to mean *very,* as in *quite good,
quite hard.*

Real. Keep expressions like *real good* and *real exciting* out of
your written English. Use *really good* and *very good.*

Reason is because. In informal usage you may hear: "The
reason I told you *is because* I can trust you." For formal
writing, revise as follows: Method 1: The reason I told
you is *that* I can trust you. [*Because* changed to *that.*]
Method 2: I told you because I can trust you. [The sentence recast.]

Should of. The term *should of* is illiterate for *should have.*
(See *Could of.*)

So. (1) Do not overuse *so* as a conjunction joining main
clauses. (See **Subordination.**) (2) Do not use *so* where
you could use *so that.* Change "I came to visit you *so*
we could have a chat" to "I came to visit you *so that*
we could have a chat." (3) Do not overuse *so* as an

intensifier: "I was *so* disappointed." "She is *so* nice, isn't she?" Try substituting *very* or *extremely.*

Sort of. (See *Kind of.*)

Strata. Use *strata* only as a plural, not as a singular noun. The singular is *stratum.* Nonstandard: He came from an extremely disadvantaged *strata* of society. Standard: He came from an extremely disadvantaged *stratum* of society.

Sure. Use *certainly* or *surely:* "I *certainly* [not *sure*] was tired."

Then, than. *Then* is sometimes a misspelling of *than. Than* is used in comparisons: They would rather die *than* surrender." *Then* means *consequently* or *as a result,* or it refers to time and means *next* or *at that time:* "If the sun is a dying star, *then* the earth is doomed to extinction." "He came, he saw, and *then* he turned around and left."

Try and. *Try and* is an informal version of *try to:* "I am going to *try and* help my neighbor." In formal English write: "I am going to *try to* help my neighbor."

Where at. In a sentence like "I know *where* he is *at,*" *at* is unnecessary and should be dropped: "I know *where* he is."

Which, who. Use *who* (or *that*), but never use *which* to refer to persons. "Here is the man *who* [not *which*] is responsible."

While. *While* is mainly a conjunction of time: "I ran *while* I still had time." Do not overwork it to mean *and, but,* or *whereas:* "I loved roses, *but* [not *while*] she preferred daisies."

Would of. The term *would of* is illiterate for *would have.* (See *Could of.*)

ELLIPSIS ——————————— ... /

In formal writing, the ellipsis – three double-spaced periods – is used only to show that you have omitted material from a *quoted* passage. (In creative writing – fiction, for example – the ellipsis is sparingly used to suggest emotion or to heighten suspense.)

Examples of the formal use of the ellipsis are as follows:

Poetry turns all things to loveliness; it exalts the beauty of that which is most beautiful, and it adds beauty to that which is most deformed; ... it subdues to union ... all irreconcilable things.
—Percy Bysshe Shelley

Use *four* double-spaced periods in the ellipsis when the material you have omitted ends a sentence:

Branshaw Manor, says the author, "lies in a little hollow with lawns across it .... The immense wind, coming from across the forest, roared overhead." [The following was omitted from the *end* of the first quoted sentence, "and pine-woods on the fringe of the dip."]

43

To show that you are omitting one or more paragraphs from a quoted passage of prose or that you are cutting at least a full line from quoted poetry, use a full line of periods:

What thou lovest well remains,
. . . .
What thou lov'st well is thy true heritage
—Ezra Pound

em ——————————— EMPHASIS

Give proper emphasis to the more important parts of the sentence and less emphasis to the less important parts.

Use the following methods for emphasizing important words or ideas.

1. *Rearrange your sentence to give the important words and phrases their proper emphasis.* The position of greatest emphasis is the *end* of your sentence. Next in emphasis is the beginning of your sentence:

   POOR EMPHASIS: We jammed into the car and started on our trip *in the morning, just after the sun rose.* [The italicized phrases are the least important elements of the sentence, but they are placed at the end, the position of most emphasis.]
   PROPER EMPHASIS: In the morning, just after the sun rose, we jammed into the car and started on our trip. [The main clause, beginning *we jammed,* is now properly emphasized.]

2. *Change the weak passive voice of the verb to the strong active voice.* (See **Passive Voice.**)

UNEMPHATIC PASSIVE VOICE: At camp, many games *were played by the children* that were not played at home.

EMPHATIC ACTIVE VOICE: At camp, *the children played* many games that they did not play at home.

3. *Underline a word or phrase for strong emphasis.* Use sparingly. Underlined words in a manuscript appear in italics *(slant type like this)* in print. Underline a word or phrase for strong emphasis only if you cannot achieve the emphasis by rephrasing or rearranging sentence parts. (See **Italics**.)

It is of course *possible* that all or any of our beliefs may be mistaken. . . . But we cannot have *reason* to reject a belief except on the ground of some other belief.

—Bertrand Russell

EXCLAMATION POINT ———— !/

Insert an exclamation point, or omit one if you have used one incorrectly. The exclamation point is used to express *strong* feeling. Do not overuse it:

PROPER USE: What a wonderful, wonderful day! [Exuberance.]

PROPER USE: Get out of here! [A brisk command.]

OVERUSE: The first baseman leaped up! He ripped the ball out of the air! The double play that followed was a cinch!

REVISION: The first baseman leaped up. He ripped the ball out of the air. The double-play that followed was a cinch. [These short, jabbing sentences are emphatic enough without exclamation points.]

frag — FRAGMENTARY SENTENCE

Change the sentence fragment to a complete sentence. You have written only a phrase or a subordinate clause, or some other *piece* of a sentence, but not a full sentence. If you can logically attach what you have written to the previous or the following sentence, do so. If not, expand your fragment into a full sentence by adding the missing element(s).

In certain types of creative writing, fragments are used effectively to suggest the frequently rapid and nongrammatical flow of thought, especially at emotional high points. But in formal, expository writing, where logic and calm are needed, sentence fragments are rarely appropriate.

The simplest sorts of fragments to correct are called *period faults*. They are sentences ended *too soon*. Usually a comma is needed in place of the faulty period. In the following examples, unjustifiable sentence fragments are in italics:

PERIOD FAULT: I do not have the steadiest hand in the world. *As you can see from my writing.*

The fragment is a subordinate clause that should be attached to the previous sentence by a comma. (For a further explanation, see **Comma**, 3.)

REVISION: I do not have the steadiest hand in the world, *as you can see from my writing.*

PERIOD FAULT: He spent some of his college years in Tucson. *A city where the weather is springlike eight months of the year.*

The fragment is an appositive. An *appositive* is a noun that renames or identifies a previous noun. In this case, the appositive *city* refers to the already named *Tucson*. Join the appositive to the first part of the sentence with a comma.

REVISION: He spent some of his college years in Tucson, *a city where the weather is springlike eight months of the year.*

In more complicated cases, fragments result when parts of a sentence are missing altogether:

FRAGMENT: She lectured on a number of occult subjects. *For example, about numerology.*

The fragment is a phrase. It is better style to make a complete sentence out of it than to add it to the previous sentence.

REVISION: She lectured on a number of occult subjects. For example, *she spoke* about numerology.

Better yet, however, would be to recast the entire idea: *She lectured on numerology and a number of other occult subjects.*

FRAGMENT: John would not make a good captain. *A good player, yes, but not always a good sport.*

The fragment here is a sentence part that needs a subject and verb. But the subject and verb were both omitted. Supply them:

REVISION: John would not make a good captain. *He is* a good player, yes, but not always a good sport.

HYPHEN  hy

Insert a hyphen (-) where indicated. The hyphen is mainly used to connect words that are to be regarded as a unit of meaning: *fire-eater, helter-skelter, rabble-rouser.* **(In many cases, usage is not generally agreed upon even among dictionaries. In order to be consistent, choose one recent dictionary and follow it.)**

The following examples illustrate special uses of hyphens, such as preventing misreading and end-of-line word division.

1. *Use a hyphen to connect modifying words before a noun when such words act as a unit of meaning:*

    - *an intelligent-looking face*
    - *nineteenth-century history* [but not in *the history of the nineteenth century*]
    - *a do-or-die attitude*
    - *behind-the-scenes dealings* [But in the sentence "There were shady dealings going on behind the scenes," no hyphens are used because *behind the scenes* comes *after* the noun.]
    - *four-, six-, and eight-cylinder cars.* [Sometimes hyphens *dangle* in a series before a noun.]

2. *Use a hyphen to prevent misreading:*

    - *a foreign-car salesman* [unless you mean *a foreign car-salesman,* a Frenchman, for example, who sells cars in his native Paris]
    - *a small-appliance store* [Such a store could be very large, indeed, but nobody would believe it if you removed the hyphen!]
    - They *re-covered* the chair. [Compare: They *recovered* the stolen chair.]

3. *Use hyphens for numbers between twenty and one hundred:* twenty-nine, sixty-two, eighty-eight (See **Numbers**.)

4. *Use a hyphen for an end-of-line word division:* hyphen-ation, not *hyphe-nation*. Divide words at the end of a full syllable. Follow the word divisions in a good dictionary, for example: sym·pa·thet·ic.

INCOMPLETE CONSTRUCTION ———————— inc

Add the word or words necessary to complete the construction you now have.

PREPOSITION OMITTED: She was greatly interested and enthusiastic about the project.

REVISED: She was greatly interested *in* and enthusiastic about the project.

VERB OMITTED: The people were all interesting and my vacation, in general, wonderful.

REVISED: The people were all interesting and my vacation, in general, *was* wonderful. [The plural verb *were*, used with *people*, does not agree with the singular noun *vacation*.]

VERB OMITTED: We never have and never shall attack without provocation.

REVISED: We never have *attacked* and never shall attack without provocation. [The auxiliary verb *have* must be followed by *attacked*.]

(See **Comparison** for other examples of incomplete constructions.)

ital ———————————— ITALICS

Underline the word or passage indicated. When printed, underlined words appear in italic or slanted type, *like this*. If you underline (or italicize) words, you are asking the reader to pay greater than usual attention to them. Frequent underlining is annoying to the eye and mind of the reader. Underline no more than is absolutely necessary—under normal circumstances, perhaps three or four times per page at most. There are four situations that call for underlining:

1. Underline the titles of books, magazines, newspapers, plays, and movies. Do not put quotation marks around them: *The Hobbit, Newsweek,* the *New York Times, Our Town, Jaws.* (For further information see **Quotation Marks**, 3.)

2. Underline foreign words and expressions: *coup d'état, al fresco, chutzpah, persona non grata.*

3. Underline words or letters if they are not used for their meaning, but as words or letters only: Add a *u* to *gaze* and you get *gauze.*

4. Underline words when strong emphasis is desired: "I'm leaving *now*," she declared, "*not* tomorrow!" (See **Emphasis**.)

NOTE: Do not underline and do not put quotation marks around the title of your own essay or composition.

LOGIC ——————————— log

Reread the marked passage, and try to discover the flaw in your language or line of reasoning. You may have failed to argue your point convincingly. Your problem may be ineffective phrasing, ineffective thinking, or both. Think through your idea again, and if it still seems worth defending, try to present it more effectively.

Many of the problems in writing that damage your logic—the clear and convincing expression of your ideas—are dealt with in this handbook under the following headings: **Abstract Expressions, Ambiguity, Coherence, Incomplete Construction, Mixed Construction, Paragraph, Shift in Point of View, Transitions, Vagueness.**

If the problem lies mainly in the *thought* rather than the expression, perhaps your difficulty falls into one of the following common categories of faulty logic:

1. Oversimplification.
2. Overgeneralization.
3. Appeal to authority.

4. Appeal to emotion.

5. Non sequitur.

1. OVERSIMPLIFICATION

You make a statement that you want your readers to believe, but you give either inadequate evidence or too simple an explanation. Few statements can be absolutely proved, but you should present *good evidence* or *sound argument* to support your point of view. Good evidence consists of concrete examples and relevant facts and figures. A sound argument recognizes and tries to deal with the complexity of most issues:

EVIDENCE MISSING: The quality of student life on campus is poor. If conditions do not improve soon, many students may leave this university. [If no examples of the poor conditions that are claimed are given, the reader has no way of judging how true that first statement might be. Supply the evidence.]

IMPROVED (EVIDENCE SUPPLIED): The quality of student life on campus is poor. *In a recent student survey, 70 percent of those polled found the food at the student cafeteria "unacceptable," 62 percent found library personnel "unhelpful," and 84 percent found their dormitories "poorly managed."* If condi-

tions do not improve soon, many students may leave this university.

COMPLEXITY UNRECOGNIZED: If families were more stable, no real narcotics problem would exist in this country. [This is an example of overly simple *cause-and-effect* reasoning. It is too simple to assume that unstable family situations *directly cause* narcotics addiction. A revised statement would avoid such a narrow cause-and-effect claim.]

IMPROVED: The instability of the family is a *factor that contributes to* the narcotics problem in this country.

2. OVERGENERALIZATION

You are overgeneralizing when you allow *no exceptions* to your rule. Other than in the natural sciences, it is hard to find general statements that apply to absolutely every known case. Learn to *qualify* (to admit exceptions to) your statements. Be wary of using words like *always, never, all, none:*

OVERGENERALIZATION: College students are interested in partying first, studying last. [Learn to use *qualifying* words such as *some, many, sometimes, often.* As it stands now, *college students* implies *all* college students without exception.]

IMPROVED: *Many* college students are interested in partying first, studying last.

OVERGENERALIZATION: In the American family, the needs and desires of the children *always* come first. [If this were true, we would not hear of most child abuse.]

IMPROVED: In the American family, the needs and desires of the children *often* come first.

3. APPEAL TO AUTHORITY

You offer no stronger backing for your point of view than the word of a presumed authority on the subject. The word of established, well-recognized authorities may be good support for what we believe. But there is a lot wrong with relying on *false* authorities. The winner of the Indianapolis

"500" is not necessarily the best authority on what beer to drink. Another problem is that even the best authorities sometimes contradict one another. What you should avoid, if at all possible, is relying on authority and nothing but authority for your beliefs:

> APPEAL TO AUTHORITY: Jogging is one of the best exercises for ensuring good health and a long life. The governor's personal physician recently said so to reporters. [The social status of the governor's physician has evidently impressed this writer tremendously. But surely there must be better evidence to be found for the benefits of jogging.]
>
> IMPROVED: *Recently published evidence that joggers have a lower incidence of cardiac problems leads me to believe that* jogging is one of the best exercises for ensuring good health and a long life.

> APPEAL TO AUTHORITY: Earth landings of flying saucers with alien beings in them have actually occurred, according to last week's *National Investigator,* and the government has for many years been suppressing news of them. [Suppose the *National Investigator* is a periodical that is not known for objective, factual reporting. Although the statement *may* be true, the *authority* quoted in support of it will prevent most readers from giving it serious consideration.]
>
> IMPROVED: *There are many unconfirmed reports that* earth landings of flying saucers with alien beings in them have actually occurred, *and it is quite possible that* the government has for many years been suppressing news of them. [There is nothing wrong with making the most outrageous statements, so long as you properly *qualify* them—as the words *unconfirmed* and *possible* help to do.]

4. APPEAL TO EMOTION

Instead of using objective evidence and rational argument, you support your views by an appeal to your readers' emotions—to their prejudices, fears, or vanities:

APPEAL TO EMOTION: Why would anyone want Klinger as president of the university? He has twice been divorced and his present wife is an alcoholic. [An appeal to many people's prejudices is substituted for an examination of Klinger's administrative credentials.]

IMPROVED: Why would anyone want Klinger as president of the university? *As we all remember, he was dismissed several years ago from his position as financial vice-president.*

APPEAL TO EMOTION: As almost any leading corporation executive will tell you, a Brooks Brothers suit is the only kind worth buying. [The appeal here is to the reader's desire for success and status and not to the quality of the suit itself.]

IMPROVED: *Although the price is high,* I prefer Brooks Brothers suits to *any others because of the excellent material and craftsmanship that go into them.*

5. NON SEQUITUR

The Latin term *non sequitur* means *it does not follow.* You move from one thought to another as if there is a logical connection between them, but there is none. (*Appeal to emotion* is a special case of *non sequitur.*) When one thought does not follow another, the reason may be, very simply, that you were hasty and left out a necessary bridge or transition. If you supply the transitional thought, the reader clearly sees the connection between the other two thoughts:

NON SEQUITUR: Because my next high school was much larger, we were allowed a longer lunch hour. [Something is missing here. What is the connection between the size of the school and the length of the lunch hour?]

IMPROVED: Because my next high school was much larger, *and the lines in the crowded cafeteria moved more slowly,* we were allowed a longer lunch hour.

(See **Coherence**.)

NON SEQUITUR: Because of an all-male student body, in class each student could be himself and act and speak natur-

ally. [This is a very jumbled and misleading statement because at least two facts or ideas are left out.]

IMPROVED: Because the student body *at my high school* was all male, *showing off for the females was strictly an after-school distraction,* and in class each student could be himself and act and speak naturally.

mm, mod ———— MISPLACED MODIFIER

Put the misplaced word or phrase in a closer or clearer relation to the word it modifies.

A *modifier* is a word or group of words that adds descriptive detail to any of four types of words in a sentence: nouns, verbs, adjectives, and adverbs. In the sentence, "He loves old cars," *old* is an adjective that modifies (describes) the noun *car*. In the sentence, "They fought bravely," *bravely* is an adverb that modifies the verb *fought*. In the sentence, "Be very careful," *very* is an adverb that modifies the adjective *careful*. In the sentence, "She swims extremely well," *extremely* is an adverb that modifies the more important adverb *well*.

Sometimes a modifier is *misplaced*. It shows up too soon or too late in a sentence to connect unmistakably with the word it modifies. In such cases confusion may result, as in the following examples:

MISPLACED: I *only* know what is right for us to do. [This sentence could mean, "I *alone* know what is right." Moving the adverb *only* makes the writer appear less arrogant.]
CLEARER: I know *only* what is right for us to do.

MISPLACED: The emperor was just and kind to people *in his way*. [It sounds as if the emperor was kind to people who were obstacles in his path.]
CLEARER: *In his way*, the emperor was just and kind to his people.

MISPLACED: He fell while he was running *into a manhole*.
CLEARER: He fell *into a manhole* while he was running.

MISPLACED: The woman who was working *quickly* swallowed her lunch. [This is a case of a *squinting* modifier, one that can modify either of two words. Does *quickly* modify *working* or *swallowed*? Most probably it modifies *swallowed*.] (See also **Ambiguity**.)

CLEARER: The woman who was working swallowed her lunch *quickly*.

mx ——— MIXED CONSTRUCTION

Change one part of the sentence to make it match the rest. Your sentence begins with one construction or figure of speech, then shifts to another that cannot logically or structurally complete the sentence:

> MIXED SENTENCE PARTS: By throwing the upper-right-hand lever is the way to stop the machine.

The two halves of this sentence do not fit together: The first part is an adverbial phrase that cannot serve as the subject. The second part, beginning with *is,* needs a noun as a subject. To correct the sentence, give it a subject in one of the following ways:

> CORRECTION 1: *Throwing* the upper-right-hand lever *is* the way to stop the machine. [Leave out the *By;* then the first clause becomes a noun phrase and the subject of the verb *is.*]
>
> CORRECTION 2: By throwing the upper-right-hand lever, *you can* stop the machine. [Change *is the way to* to *you can.* Now *you* is the subject of the sentence and the adverbial clause *By throwing . . . ,* modifies the verb *can stop.*]

> MIXED SENTENCE PARTS: *The reason* so few professors seek employment at this college *is because* we are located so far from any metropolitan center. [*Because* begins an adverbial clause that many writers wrongly put to work as a *noun.* Change the adverbial clause to a noun clause. *The reason . . . is because* becomes *The reason . . . is that.*]
>
> CORRECTION: *The reason* so few professors seek employment at this college *is that* we are located so far from any metropolitan center.

> MIXED SENTENCE PARTS: *Just because* she is rich is no reason to suppose she is happy.

This sentence has the same type of error as the previous one, except in reverse. This typical *just because* sentence forces an adverb clause–*because he is rich*–to serve as the subject. Subjects ought to be nouns, noun clauses, or other types of *noun* constructions. The simplest correction changes the adverbial clause into a noun clause: *Just because* becomes *The simple fact that* or *The mere fact that*.

CORRECTION: *The mere fact that* she is rich is no reason to suppose she is happy.

MIXED SENTENCE PARTS: Now, and not next month, is *when* we should write letters to our legislators.

The *is when* and *is because* constructions are similar: Adverbs are forced to do the job of nouns. Correct most *is when* sentences simply by striking out *is when* and switching the two halves of the sentence around:

CORRECTION: We should write letters to our legislators now, and not next month.

MIXED METAPHORS: The *wheels* of fate moved their grimy *hands*. [Do *wheels* have *hands?* As you can see, mixing metaphors (figures of speech) can result in an absurd image–funny, but not intentionally so.]

MIXED METAPHORS: A *tongue* of land jutted out from the *foot* of the cliff. [It is absurd to imagine a *foot* sticking out its *tongue.*]

NUMBERS ———————— num

1. **Spell out any figures that can be spoken in one or two words: *thirty, fifty-five, three hundred, two million.***
2. **Use numerals for any sum that must be expressed in three or more words: *172, 307, 1,002.***

   EXCEPTION: Spell out figures that begin a sentence: *Three hundred sixty-eight* students work part time.

¶ ———————————— PARAGRAPH

Begin a new paragraph at the place marked. In most writing, the first line of a paragraph is *indented,* that is, begins several spaces to the right of where a line usually begins. In special cases, paragraphs can be indicated by blank lines between blocks of print, or by introductory symbols such as an asterisk (*), bullet (•), or number.

The beginning of each new paragraph marks a new stage in the development of your essay. Just as sentences are the largest subunits of a paragraph, so paragraphs are the largest subunits of your essay. In formal writing, a paragraph does not begin and end just anywhere, as if the writer were playing Pin-the-Tail-on-the-Donkey. The main idea, or topic, of an essay needs to be developed in each of its important *aspects,* and a new paragraph signals the shift to a new aspect of the discussion. (If your topic is broad enough and your essay long enough, each of the main aspects may be broken down into two or more sections, or paragraphs.) If, for example, you were writing a short essay on the types of teachers you have known and you end up writing about five specific types, you may decide to write an introductory paragraph briefly mentioning your purpose and the five types you will treat. Then, you will probably devote *one paragraph* to a description (with examples) of *each type.* Your essay would, therefore, be divided into at least six paragraphs.

The main idea of each paragraph is usually found in one sentence called the topic sentence. (The theme of the whole essay is usually found in the first paragraph and is called the *thesis statement.*) A paragraph consists of a topic sentence, or main idea, plus a number of sentences that *develop* that main idea in some satisfactory way through a *logical argument,* or a series of *details* or *examples,* or any combination of these methods. The topic sentence is usually the first one in a paragraph, although it sometimes appears at the end, as a summary of details or examples that come before it.

There are three main organizational features to a well-structured paragraph:

1. *Unity*, the relevance of all sentences to the topic sentence. The avoidance of digressions–wandering from the paragraph topic.
2. *Development*, elaboration of the main idea with enough details, examples, arguments, and so forth, to give the impression of full or adequate treatment.
3. *Coherence*, the connection between one sentence and the next in a logical pattern.

The use of linking devices is an essential means of achieving coherence. There are four main types of linking devices:

1. Transitional words or phrases.
2. Repetition of key words or ideas.
3. Pronouns.
4. Demonstrative adjectives (*this, that, these, those*).

(For more information see **Coherence** and **Transitions**.)

EXAMPLE: **One of the most significant changes in American family lifestyles in recent years has been the increase in the number of working women** [Topic sentence]. Each year more and more are joining the ranks of the employed in search of personal fulfillment and financial independence. In fact, [Trans. Phr.] over half of the adult female population is now in the labor force [Rep. idea]. Of particular importance to the family lifestyle [Rep. key words] is the fact that half of all children under eighteen now have working mothers. The Census Bureau reported that 45 percent of all mothers [Rep. key word] of preschool children are presently working. That [Demon. adj.] figure [Rep. idea] is four times higher than it was just thirty years ago.

This increase in the number of working women has caused a redefinition of family roles. [Trans. sentence linking ¶s]. **One important change is that husbands and children are expected to do more around the house.** In many households children are expected not only to do [Rep. key idea] the dishes and clean their rooms, but also to do the family grocery shopping, cook some of the meals, and help care for the younger children. And because a working woman contributes to the family's economic welfare, [Rep. key idea] husbands are beginning to share in what was once considered "woman's work": babysitting, cooking, and doing the laundry.

paral, // ——— PARALLELISM

When two or more sentence elements are equally important in content and function, make them alike in grammatical form. *Parallelism* **is the matching of sentence elements with one another: subject with subject, verb with verb, object with object, indirect object with indirect object, modifier with modifier. Usually, when these like sentence elements appear in a pair or a series, they are connected with coordinating conjunctions:**

> POOR: I enjoy going to movies, listening to music, and cards.
>
> REVISION 1: I enjoy *going* to movies, *listening* to music, and *playing* cards.

The verb is *enjoy,* and its objects are *going, listening,* and *playing.* Since these sentence elements are all objects, they should be in the same form. In this case the objects should all be gerunds: -ing words used as nouns.

> REVISION 2: I enjoy *movies, music,* and *cards.*

This series is also parallel because the three objects–*movies, music,* and *cards*–are all nouns. However, these nouns are not as specific as the gerunds in the first revised sentence.

POOR: The opinion of one off-beat columnist is that the mayor is adept at underhand dealings profitable only to himself, and we should therefore throw him out of office.

REVISED: The opinion of one off-beat columnist is *that* the mayor is adept at underhand dealings profitable only to himself and *that* we should therefore throw him out of office.

The second *that* makes it clear that the opinion that follows is solely the columnist's and does not belong to the writer of the sentence. You see how important clear parallelism can be.

POOR: He always plays the piano with ease, with confidence, and takes pleasure in it.

REVISED: He always plays the piano *with ease, with confidence,* and *with pleasure.*

In the revised sentence we have a series of parallel prepositional phrases. Because the three phrases modify the same verb–*plays*–they should be parallel.

PARENTHESES ———— paren, ()

Use parentheses to enclose material that is clearly additional commentary or detail and not essential to the meaning of the sentence. Whatever is enclosed in parentheses appears relatively unimportant to the reader. Use parentheses sparingly; never use them when you can use commas instead.

Effective Use of Parentheses

- I walked right up to him (no one was with him at the time) and told him what we had decided.
- Last week she came up with a brilliant new idea (the seeds of it had been ripening in her mind for months) only to see it rejected as absurd by the committee.

Ineffective Use of Parentheses

- His brother told him (John) not to annoy him (Allen) anymore.

You should not compensate for poor reference of pronouns by using explanatory parentheses. The sentence needs rewriting to achieve a smooth style and clear meaning: *His brother told John not to annoy Allen anymore.*

- Some critics think that atmospheric pollution (not the population explosion) is the more serious challenge to human survival.

Commas are better than parentheses to set off this relatively important part of the sentence.

PASSIVE VOICE ———————— pass

Make your writing more direct by changing the verb from the passive voice to the active voice. (See *Emphasis*.)

Verbs that take a direct object are in the *active voice:*

ACTIVE: The referee blew the whistle. [The word *whistle* is the direct object of *blew*, a verb in the active voice.]

When the direct object becomes the subject, the verb changes to a form of the verb *to be* plus a past participle and is said to be in the *passive voice:*

PASSIVE: The whistle was blown. [The word *whistle* in the previous example was a direct object, but now it is the subject. The verb *was blown*–a form of *to be* plus a past participle–is in the *passive* voice.]

Notice how the following sentences are more direct in the active voice:

WEAK PASSIVE VOICE: With the changing of seasons there comes a change in the type of clothing *to be worn.*
DIRECT ACTIVE VOICE: With the changing of seasons there comes a change in the type of clothing *people wear.* [Even better: *With the changing of the seasons people change the type of clothing they wear.*]

PASSIVE: In the fall, cotton clothes *are stored away* by families.
ACTIVE: In the fall, *families store away* their cotton clothes.

PASSIVE: I am sure this *can be done* by us if the money *can be found.*
ACTIVE: I am sure *we can do* this if *we can find* the money.

Effective Uses of the Passive Voice

The passive voice may be used if the receiver of the action, or the action itself, is more important than the doer:

- The mayor of New York City *was bitten* today by a horse. [The *receiver* of the biting, the mayor of New York, gets top billing in this sentence.]
- The restaurant fire was started by a dripping panful of hot grease. [The *action*, the fire, is of more interest than who or what started it.]

The passive voice may be used if the doer of the action is unknown:

- Some years ago a treasure-laden Spanish galleon *was recovered* not far from the coast of Florida. [The writer may not know who recovered it or simply may not find that detail worth mentioning.]

Except in cases when the passive voice is needed, a careful writer will avoid passive voice constructions because they often lead to weak, roundabout, wordy sentences.

pro ——— PRONOUN REFERENCE

Make the pronoun you have used clearly refer to a previous noun (its antecedent).

1. DANGLING PRONOUNS

Certain pronouns, especially *which, this,* and *it,* are sometimes found to be *dangling* in a sentence because they simply have no antecedent–no noun–within reach for them to refer to. Dangling pronouns usually mean well. Often, they try to refer to a whole previous idea, but the idea has not been cast in the form of a noun. To revise the idea, restate it in the form of a noun:

UNCLEAR REFERENCE: He felt extremely angry toward her, which made it difficult for him to speak to her.

The dangling pronoun *which* is used–impossibly–to refer to the whole preceding main clause. It lacks an *antecedent*, a *noun* to refer to. Revise the idea in either of two ways: (1) Change the *which* part of the sentence to fit the main clause. (2) Change the main clause to fit the *which* part of the sentence.

> REVISION 1: He felt extremely angry toward her. *His attitude* made it difficult for him to speak to her. [This solution turns one sentence into two.]
>
> REVISION 2: His anger toward her reached an *extreme* that made it difficult for him to speak to her. [*That* now clearly refers to the noun *extreme*.]

> UNCLEAR REFERENCE: Anthony played varsity football, chaired the history club, spoke fluent Italian, and drew cartoons for the college newspaper. *This* explains why the student body elected him president.

The pronoun *this* is forced to refer to the whole preceding sentence. To revise, combine the pronoun *this* with a noun, or perhaps a more descriptive noun phrase, which sums up the ideas of the whole previous sentence.

> REVISION: Anthony played varsity football, chaired the history club, spoke fluent Italian, and drew cartoons for the college newspaper. *This record of all-round excellence* explains why the student body elected him president.

> UNCLEAR REFERENCE: How can you not be happy to see *the leaves appear* in the spring and the difference *it* makes in everything about you? [The pronoun *it* awkwardly refers to the whole previous clause, *the leaves appear in the spring.*]
>
> REVISION: How can you not be happy to see *the appearance of the leaves* in the spring and the difference *it* makes in everything about you? [*It* now refers to the noun *appearance.*]

> UNCLEAR REFERENCE: *It said* in last week's *Times* that there was no foreseeable end to inflation.

Similar to this kind of sentence is the one that begins, *They said on the radio that* . . . The *it*–or *they*–implies a subject that is not stated. In formal writing, avoid this kind of construction. A simple revision uses *I read* or *I heard* to begin such a sentence.

REVISION: *I read* in last week's *Times* that there was no foreseeable end to inflation.

2. AMBIGUOUS PRONOUNS

Some pronouns refer *ambiguously* to either of two previous nouns. Pronouns should refer to one noun and one noun only. Your job is to remove the ambiguity. Reduce your pronoun's workload to one noun that it clearly refers to. (See **Ambiguity**.)

AMBIGUOUS REFERENCE: When John spoke to Peter, he said he doubted that *he* would be invited to the party. [Does the last *he* refer to John or Peter?]

REVISION: When John spoke to Peter, he said, "I doubt that I will be invited to the party." [The use of direct quotation is the simplest way to solve this sort of reference problem.]

AMBIGUOUS REFERENCE: Even if the salesperson persuades you to purchase an item, do not sign anything. Ask her to leave the contract with you so that you and your wife may read it thoroughly. If *she* will not *do it*, show her the door. [In the last sentence, the ambiguous use of *she* and *it* can lead to a rather amusing interpretation.]

REVISION: Even if the salesperson persuades you to purchase an item, do not sign anything. Ask her to leave the contract with you so that you and your wife may read it thoroughly. If the *salesperson* will not *leave it with you*, show her the door. [It is not enough to change *she* to *salesperson*. The dangling *it* in *do it* has no noun to attach to. It is made to refer to either of two verb–object combinations: *leave the contract* or *read it*. To clarify, change *do it* to *leave it with you*.]

QUOTATION MARKS — quot, "/"

Use quotation marks to set off (1) directly quoted words, (2) words used in an unusual way, and (3) the titles of subunits of a book or magazine—a chapter, story, poem, and so on.

The following instructions show when and how to use a pair of quotation marks (" ").

WHEN TO USE QUOTATION MARKS

1. *Use quotation marks to enclose a passage of directly quoted words:*

- The flight attendant said, "Fasten your seat belts, please."
- In his *Essay on Man*, Alexander Pope says, "Hope springs eternal in the human breast."

CAUTION: Do not use quotation marks for *indirect* quotations. An indirect quotation is a second-hand report of what someone said, and it is often introduced by the word *that:*

MISUSE: My brother said that "he was unhappy about the outcome."
REVISION: My brother said that he was unhappy about the outcome. [Remove the quotation marks. Quotation marks could be used around the words in this sentence that are quoted: My brother said that he was "unhappy about the outcome." Or a complete direct quotation could be used: My brother said, "*I am* unhappy about the outcome."]

Keep identification of the speaker, such as *he said* or *she said*, outside of the quotation marks:

- "I suppose," *he remarked*, "that success comes only with time." [Since the quoted passage is one complete sentence, the interrupting words are set off by commas and not followed by a period or semicolon.]

- "I understand the plan," *Jim said.* "I think it might work." [In this case, two separate sentences are quoted. *Jim said* must be followed by a period, for it marks the end of one quoted sentence.]

When quoting long prose passages do not use quotation marks. Instead, indent the entire passage five spaces to the right (a few more spaces for the first line of a paragraph) and single space if you are typing. The following example is from a student research paper.

The author sums up in a nutshell the basic conditions that have shaped Spain's cultural development:

> Spain is a world apart from the rest of Europe, separated by climatic differences and isolated in time as well as in space. Bounded by water on three sides, and on the fourth cut off by the barrier of the Pyrenees, she was for three hundred years, from the VIIIth to the XIth centuries, virtually under the domination of an oriental power—that of the Moors, whose culture was not only more advanced than that of any part of Europe, but also profoundly different from any European civilization.
>
> —Enriqueta Harris
> *Spanish Painting*

When quoting one or two lines of poetry, follow the example for a directly quoted passage:

- Wallace Stevens is playing a musical joke when he writes, "Chieftain Iffucan of Azcan in caftan/ Of tan with henna hackles, halt!" [Note the slash used to show the line end.]

When quoting more than two lines of poetry, do not use quotation marks. Simply indent the whole passage as for long prose quotations, single space if typing, and reproduce the original as it stands.

2. *Use quotation marks to emphasize words used in an unusual sense:*

   • In the printing trade, an engraved plate is called a "cut."

   NOTE: Do not use quotation marks to ask acceptance for lazy, imprecise language of your own:

   • In spite of Jerry's "goofing off," he was generally regarded as a very "sharp" character.

3. *Use quotation marks to set off the titles of chapters of a book; episodes of a TV or radio series; and the titles of articles, short stories, and poems published as* part *of a complete book, magazine, or newspaper:*

   • One of my favorite stories is Hemingway's "The Killers."

   The title of the whole book is underlined, or italicized, whereas the chapter title is in quotation marks:

   • When you read *Sister Carrie*, pay careful attention to the first chapter, "The Magnet Attracting: A Waif Amid Forces."

   The *series* title of a TV or radio show is underlined, whereas the title of an individual episode is in quotation marks:

   • Last week I watched an excellent program called "The Winged World" on *Best of the National Geographic Specials.*

   NOTE: Do *not* use quotation marks around the title of your *own* essay. Do not underline your own title, either. To set it off clearly from the beginning of your essay, just skip a line or two between your title and your first paragraph.

How to Use Quotation Marks With Other Punctuation

Place periods and commas inside *closing quotation marks:*

- Shakespeare said, "Unquiet meals make ill digestions."
- Francis Bacon remarked that "the monuments of wit survive the monuments of power," and I wholly agree with him.

Place colons and semicolons outside *closing quotations marks:*

- We had arrived at "the moment of truth": The matador extended his sword for the finishing stroke.
- I know that "to err is human"; yet fifteen errors in one ball game is too much to forgive.

Place question marks and exclamation points inside *closing quotation marks* only *if they are a part of the quoted passage:*

- I asked her, "Is dinner ready?"
- He shouted, "Advance or I'll fire!"

Place such marks outside the quotation marks if they are *not* part of the quoted passage:

- Did I just hear you say, "Dinner is ready"?
- Stop saying "yes"!

In direct quotations, avoid the extra comma or period after a closing quotation mark:

AVOID: "Well, well!", he said. [Remove the comma.]
BETTER: "Well, well!" he said.

AVOID: He asked, "What's your name?". [Remove the period.]
BETTER: He asked, "What's your name?"

Use single quotation marks (' ') to set off a quotation within a quotation:

- "When Caesar said 'I came, I saw, I conquered,'" my history teacher declared, "little did he know that he had invented the telegram."

If you quote an essay title that quotes another title, use single quotation marks for the quoted title within the title:

- I just read a journal article about Robert Frost and his poem "Two Tramps in Mud Time." The title of the article is "Frost and the Work Ethic: 'Two Tramps in Mud Time.'"

In the journal, the title has no quotation marks around it, but the title of the poem it quotes is set in *double* quotation marks:

- Frost and the Work Ethic: "Two Tramps in Mud Time."

REPETITION ——————— rep

Do not awkwardly repeat the same word or idea you have used before. (See *Wordiness*.) The more serious problem is the repetition of the same idea — whether in similar form or not — throughout the whole length of a composition. (See *Paragraph*.) Such repetition suggests that you have little to say but feel pressured to fill up space. The following examples show awkward uses of repetition and correction of the awkwardness:

REPETITION: A cool breeze was *blowing*, and the brownish gold leaves were being *blown* about by the wind.

Change *blown* to *swept,* or find some other good synonym. Sometimes, as in this case, the sentence would be better if it were condensed. There is no need to refer to the *breeze* again, even by the synonym *wind:*

REVISION: The brownish gold leaves were being swept about by the cool breeze.

REPETITION: The air was too cold, *and* while I was asleep it chilled me, *and* when I awoke my bones felt stiff. [Eliminate one of the *and's.*]
REVISION: The air was too cold. While I was asleep it chilled me, and when I awoke my bones felt stiff.

REPETITION: I want to earn a college degree *because* I would like many options to remain open to me in the future *because* rapid technological changes leave people of meager education at a great disadvantage. [Avoid the *because . . . because* construction.]
REVISION: I want to earn a college degree because I would like many options to remain open to me in the future. Rapid technological changes leave people of meager education at a great disadvantage.

REPETITION: The steam could be seen rising from the radiator. *The steam* turned to frost on the windowpane. [Delete the second *steam,* and combine the two sentences.]
REVISION: The steam rising from the radiator turned to frost on the windowpane.

REPETITION: He *walked up and down* and kept pacing about the room.
REVISION: He kept pacing about the room. [Avoid repeating the same idea.]

Repetition is not always bad. (See **Parallelism.**) Repetition of words or ideas can be used deliberately to arouse emotion or aid memory. We find such conscious repetition in the most varied kinds of communication, from commercial advertising and political propaganda to poetry and oratory. The last major speech of Martin Luther King, Jr., is unforgettable because of the mounting repetitions, "I have a dream. . . ." And in the Bible, Ecclesiastes 3:1–3, the repetitions sound with a poetic beat: "To every thing there is a season, and a time to every purpose under the heaven. A time to be born, and a time to die; A time to plant, and a time to pluck up that which is planted; A time to kill, and a time to heal. . . ."

RUN-ON SENTENCE ———— RO

Do not run one sentence into the next unless you separate them with proper punctuation or a coordinating conjunction. End the first sentence with a period or other end-of-sentence punctuation such as a question mark or exclamation point, and begin the next sentence with a capital letter. A semicolon will sometimes work better than a period or conjunction. (See *Semicolon*, 2.) In any case, do *not* join two sentences with only a comma. Although this comma error is sometimes called a run-on sentence, it is usually referred to as a *comma splice*. (See *Comma Splice*):

RUN-ON: The Chinese are wonderful Ping-Pong players they really deserve their world-champion status.
REVISION: The Chinese are wonderful Ping-Pong players. They really deserve their world-champion status.

RUN-ON: She put on her bathing cap then she plunged into the water.
REVISION 1: She put on her bathing cap. Then she plunged into the water.

Although a period is correct, a semicolon would probably be better between *cap* and *then*. (Look up the use of semicolons before conjunctive adverbs like *then, however,* and *therefore* under **Comma Splice**.)

REVISION 2: She put on her bathing cap, then plunged into the water.

Use fewer words wherever convenient. By eliminating the second *she* and adding a comma after *cap*, we are left with a single, smooth sentence.

RUN-ON: The snow fell all night in the morning the air was crystal clear.

REVISION 1: The snow fell all night. In the morning the air was crystal clear.

REVISION 2: The snow fell all night, *but* in the morning the air was crystal clear.

Sometimes a comma and a coordinating conjunction such as *but* or *and* make a smoother sentence. (See **Comma,** 1.)

NOTE: When sentences are short, they may be joined with a coordinating conjunction and no punctuation:

● He ran *and* she hid.

SEMICOLON ———————— semi

1. **Use the semicolon to connect two main clauses when they are closely related in idea.**
2. **Use the semicolon to separate sentence elements equal in rank when they contain commas.**

1. CONNECTING INDEPENDENT CLAUSES

Use the semicolon to connect two related, complete sentences, generally when they are not connected with a coordinating conjunction such as *and, but, for, or, nor*:

- It is not so much the threatening weather that concerns me; it is the dilapidated condition of the ship. [The ideas are closely related.]

Also use the semicolon between main clauses connected by certain conjunctive adverbs, such as *however, therefore, then, similarly, likewise*. (See **Comma Splice**.)

- I would like to attend the conference; *however,* I have a prior appointment that I am unable to cancel.

Do not use the semicolon between a main clause and a phrase or subordinate clause:

AVOID: I do not like to eat orange peels; although I admit that in marmalade they are quite good. [Remove the semicolon.]

BETTER: I do not like to eat orange peels although I admit that in marmalade they are quite good. [No punctuation is normally needed between a main and a subordinate clause.]

2. SEPARATING EQUAL ELEMENTS

Use the semicolon to show the main divisions in equal sentence elements containing commas:

> I introduced him to Jack Kreel, the president; Will Baum, the vice-president; and Herb Dunn, the treasurer.

sexist ——— SEXIST EXPRESSION

Avoid terms that refer to only one sex if they *unfairly* exclude the other. Whenever possible, choose pronouns and occupational titles that reflect equal treatment of the sexes.

1. SEXIST PRONOUNS

A special problem in the use of pronouns may occur when the following words are used as antecedents: *each, every, everyone, everybody, everything, someone, somebody, anyone, anybody, no one, nobody, either, neither, another.* Although they may occur in a sentence as antecedents, these words are themselves singular pronouns and should be referred to by singular pronouns.

> **EXAMPLE:** *Each* of us knows *his* job. (The use of *his* assumes that *us* consists entirely of males.)
> **EXAMPLE:** *Each* of the women presented *her* opinion.

NOTE: When any of these antecedents stands for a group of both men and women, you have several options:

A. You may use a double pronoun: Each of us knows *his* or *her* job well. Because double references can get cumbersome if overused, try these alternate ways to represent both male and female in a group.

B. Leave out the pronouns entirely where possible:

CORRECT: Everyone made *his* or *her* presentation.
BETTER: Everyone made a presentation.

C. Use plurals where possible:

CORRECT: Everyone made *his* or *her* presentation.
BETTER: *All managers* made *their* presentations.

D. When omitting the pronouns or using the plural is not possible, write or rewrite to avoid implying that the group you are referring to, which actually includes both men and women, is composed exclusively of men:

MISLEADING: Anyone, if *he* works hard enough, can succeed.
BETTER: Anyone *who* works hard enough can succeed.

2. SEXIST JOB TITLES

Avoid labeling an occupation as belonging particularly to one sex. If you use the word *foreman*, for instance, you may suggest to your readers—even without meaning to—that you assume anyone in charge of a work crew to be a male. Although such language is in common use, many people consider it sexist, implying prejudice against one of the sexes. Instead of *foreman* you might use a sexually neutral term like *supervisor* or *section head*. Some common sexist expressions and their nondiscriminatory alternatives follow:

SEXIST	ALTERNATIVE
Businessman	Business executive, business owner, business person, company head, manufacturer, wholesaler
Congressman	Representative
Fireman	Firefighter
Foreman	Supervisor
Housewife	Housekeeper
Manpower	Workers, work force
Repairman	Service technician
Salesman	Sales representative, salesperson
Workman	Worker, laborer, employee

shift — SHIFT IN POINT OF VIEW

1. **Make the pronouns in your sentences agree in *number* and *person*.**
2. **Make the verbs in your sentences agree in *tense*, *mood*, and *voice*.**
3. **Do not carelessly present as your own statements those that should be attributed to others.**

1. PRONOUN SHIFTS

Avoid Shifts in Number

A shift in pronoun number occurs when you shift between singular and plural pronouns while referring to the same noun:

> SHIFT: During the sixties women gained more control over their roles in society than they previously possessed. Now is no time for *her* to give up in *her* struggle for equal rights.
>
> REVISED: During the sixties women gained more control over their roles in society than they previously possessed. Now is no time for *them* to give up in *their* struggle for equal rights.

(See **Agreement**, 2.)

Avoid Shifts in Person

The personal pronouns are classified as *first-*, *second-*, and *third-person* pronouns (singular or plural). (See **Case.**) Examples of first-person pronouns are *I, me, we, our.* Second-person pronouns include *you, your, yours.* Third-person pronouns include *he, she, it, one, they.* Avoid needless shifts in person not only within the same sentence but from sentence to sentence and from paragraph to paragraph throughout the entire essay:

> SHIFT: If *one* stops to watch them work, *you* are greeted with a smile.

REVISION 1: If *one* stops to watch them work, *one* is greeted with a smile. [Avoid frequent use of the impersonal *one*. It can make your style seem stiff.]

REVISION 2: If *you* stop to watch them work, *you* are greeted with a smile.

2. VERB SHIFTS

Avoid Shifts in Tense

A verb's tense tells your reader when the action takes place. (See **Tense**.) If you shift unnecessarily, for instance, from the past to the present, you may confuse your reader. Avoid unnecessary shifts in tense not only within the same sentence but from sentence to sentence and paragraph to paragraph throughout an essay:

SHIFT: He *rushed* to catch his train but *misses* it by half a minute. [A needless shift from the past–*rushed*–to the present–*misses*.]

REVISED: He *rushed* to catch his train but *missed* it by half a minute.

Avoid Shifts in Mood

English has three verb moods: the *indicative*, the *imperative*, and the *subjunctive*. Most of the time, we speak and write in the indicative mood–the forms used for making declarative statements such as "I *work* on weekends." We use the *imperative* mood when we issue commands (to an implied you): "*Work faster.*" The most common mood-shift *error* is from the imperative to the indicative:

SHIFT: *Be* sure to visit the science exhibition, and then you *should go* to the art show. [*Be* is the imperative; *should go* is the indicative.]

REVISED: *Be* sure to visit the science exhibition, and then *go* to the art show. [Both verbs, *be* and *go*, are now in the imperative mood.]

Occasionally, we use the *subjunctive* mood–when we discuss possibilities instead of facts and when we use certain stock

phrases like *"Be* that as it may." Use the subjunctive to discuss future events that are unlikely to happen:

INCORRECT: If I *was* rich, I would be happy.
CORRECT: If I *were* rich, I would be happy.

Avoid Shifts in Voice

Avoid changing from the active voice to the passive voice when your subject is still active. (See **Passive Voice**.) Often there is no need to change the subject from clause to clause within the same sentence:

SHIFT: *We* predicted the results more easily after the *margin of error* had been reduced. [Who reduced the margin of error?]
REVISED: *We* predicted the results more easily after *we* had reduced the margin of error.

3. SHIFTS IN THE ATTRIBUTION OF STATEMENTS

Be Clear About Who Is Saying What

Make sure that when you present the thoughts of others, the reader cannot take them as your own statements or opinions. Only a few words of attribution are needed for clarification:

SHIFT: In Eudora Welty's "Petrified Man," women are portrayed as victims of Hollywood-inspired fantasy. *The real men in their lives are all hindrances, millstones, and rapists.* [The italicized sentence appears to be the opinion of the student who wrote this passage.]

REVISED: In Eudora Welty's "Petrified Man," women are portrayed as victims of Hollywood-inspired fantasy. *The female characters feel that* the real men in their lives are all hindrances, millstones, and rapists. [Addition of the italicized words makes it clear that the opinion that follows is not the student's own but belongs to the characters in Welty's story.]

SPLIT INFINITIVE ——————— split

Do not split infinitives unnecessarily. *To speak, to go, to think* are infinitives. For example, you split the infinitive *to speak* when you place a word or words between *to* and *speak: to hastily speak* or *to now and then speak*. In formal writ-

ing, split infinitives are now acceptable if they read *smoothly*. Sometimes it is less awkward to split an infinitive than not to split it, but that is not often the case:

UNACCEPTABLE: He foolishly tried *to*, without studying at all, *pass* the chemistry final.

REVISED: He foolishly tried *to pass* the chemistry final without studying at all.

UNACCEPTABLE: He manages *to* usually *bore* people to death.

REVISED: He usually manages *to bore* people to death.

ACCEPTABLE: He managed *to* completely *undermine* the work of the committee. [If you try to place *completely* else-where–before *to*, after *undermine*, or after *committee*–the sentence will not read as smoothly as it does *with* the split infinitive.]

sub ——————— SUBORDINATION

Emphasize important ideas by keeping them as main clauses. Change lesser ideas into sub-ordinate clauses, phrases, and even single words where possible. (See *Variety in Sentence Patterns*.)

COORDINATE SENTENCE STRUCTURE

In sentence structure, *subordination* is the opposite of *coordina-tion*. *Coordination* is the use of word groups that are structur-ally equal to express ideas that are equal in importance. Julius Caesar's "I came, I saw, I conquered" is a good example of main clauses arranged in a coordinate series. More typically, coordinate structures are joined by any of the following words, which are called coordinating conjunctions: *and, but, or, nor, for, yet, so*. For example, "I jog *and* I swim, *but* I do not play tennis."

SUBORDINATE SENTENCE STRUCTURE

Subordination is the use of word groups that are structurally unequal to express ideas that are unequal in importance: "I read the book because I liked the movie." Here the main idea is in the *main* clause, *I read the book,* and the less important, or subordinate, idea is in the *subordinate* clause *because I liked the movie.* The main clause, containing the main idea, can stand alone as a sentence: *I read the book;* but the subordinate clause, containing the less important idea, cannot.

Subordinate clauses begin with *subordinators*–subordinating conjunctions or relative pronouns. Here is a list of common subordinators:

SUBORDINATING CONJUNCTIONS: after, although, as, as if, as long as, as soon as, as though, because, before, even though, if, in order that, no matter how, once, provided, since, so that, though, unless, until, when, whenever, where, wherever, while, why.

RELATIVE PRONOUNS: that, what, which, who, whoever, whom, whomever, whose.

STRINGY SENTENCES: Do not use coordination–stringing ideas together with *and* or *so*–when subordination would better express the relationship of the ideas.

STRINGY: I saw the movie three times *and* I realized I always found it more fascinating each time, *so* I finally read the book.
BETTER: I finally read the book *because, after seeing* the movie three times, I realized I always found it more fascinating each time.

CHOPPY SENTENCES

Another form of abusing coordination is writing a series of short, choppy sentences even though the ideas are *not* of equal importance:

CHOPPY: People were bored. We became irritable. The picnic broke up early.

If we use *subordination,* however, we can show more clearly how these ideas are connected and express them in one smooth sentence:

BETTER: Becoming irritable out of sheer boredom, we broke up our picnic early.

(See **Choppy Sentences.**)

Further examples of sentences requiring the use of subordination follow:

STRINGY: John's employer did not care for him, *so* she refused to write him a letter of recommendation. [Two equally emphatic main clauses.]

BETTER: *Because* John's employer did not care for him, *she* refused to write him a letter of recommendation. [The first main clause, less emphatic than the second, is changed into a subordinate clause beginning with *because.*]

CHOPPY: She was exhausted. She had been swimming too long and was doubled up by a sudden cramp. She shouted for help. [This is an awkward series of choppy sentences.]

BETTER: Exhausted from swimming too long *and* doubled up by a sudden cramp, she shouted for help. [The first two sentences are turned into phrases.]

STRINGY: The moon *was glowing, and it* looked like the face of a snowman.

BETTER: The *glowing* moon looked like the face of a snowman. [The first main clause is condensed into the single word *glowing.*]

T —————————————— TENSE

1. Check to see whether you are using the proper sequence of tenses. One of the verbs

in your sentence may not be in the correct time relation with the other(s).

2. **Use your dictionary to find the correct forms of irregular verbs (for example, *choose*, *chose*, *chosen*).**

3. **Do not shift tenses without good reason. (See *Shift in Point of View*, 2.)**

Tense is the form of a verb that tells your reader the *time*–past, present, or future–that the action takes place. The verb *form* is the clue to the time. Here are three tense forms of the verb *work*: present (I *work*, he *works*); past (he *worked*); future (he *will work*).

1. SEQUENCE OF TENSES

If the time when an action takes place is the *same* in both the main clause and the subordinate clause, then the tense of both verbs must be the same:

- When she *arrived*, the crowd *greeted* her with a long ovation.
- As he slowly *turns*, he *balances* himself with his arms.

If the action in the subordinate clause takes place before that in the main clause, put the subordinate verb in the appropriate past tense:

- I *hear* that he *has worked* wonders.

The main verb, *hear,* is in the present tense; the subordinate verb, *has worked,* is in the present perfect tense. The present perfect tense expresses a time earlier than the present.

- I *heard* that he *had worked* wonders.

The past perfect, *had worked,* expresses a time prior to some understood time in the past. This *understood* past time is expressed by the simple past tense, *heard.*

When you are expressing a *permanent* fact, always use the present tense:

- I was informed that penicillin *works* wonders. [Use *works,* not *worked.*]

Keep an infinitive in the present tense if it expresses the same time as the action of the main verb; keep it in the past tense if it expresses a time before the action of the main verb:

- I would have liked *to go* with you.
- I would like *to go* with you.

In both these cases, although the main verb differs in tense, the present infinitive concerns *going* at the same time that the *liking* or desire to go is expressed.

- I would like *to have gone* with you.

Here the past infinitive is used because the wish in the present concerns an action already completed in the past.

OVERKILL: I would *have liked* to *have gone* with you.

Do not use the past infinitive together with the past tense of the main verb. Use one or the other, as shown in the earlier examples, but not both at the same time.

2. IRREGULAR VERBS

Most English verbs are *regular*, forming their past tense and past participle with *-ed*: I *waited*, I have *waited*. With a regular verb like *wait*, once you know the present tense, you know all the other tenses. There is a troublesome group of *irregular* verbs, however, whose present tense (I *break*) is no clue to the past tense (I *broke*) or to the compound past tenses formed with the past participle (I have *broken: broken* is the past participle).

If you are in doubt about the past tense forms of a verb, look up the verb in the dictionary under its present tense form (*bite*, for example) and you will find the past tense (*bit*) and past participle (*bitten*) listed in order right after it. Here is a list of some of the most frequently misused irregular verbs:

PRESENT	PAST	PAST PARTICIPLE
I *blow*	I *blew*	I have *blown*
I *bring*	I *brought*	I have *brought*
I *burst*	I *burst*	I have *burst*
I *do*	I *did*	I have *done*
I *drink*	I *drank*	I have *drunk*
I *drive*	I *drove*	I have *driven*
I *eat*	I *ate*	I have *eaten*
I *forbid*	I *forbade*	I have *forbidden*
I *go*	I *went*	I have *gone*
I *lay* (bricks)	I *laid* (bricks)	I have *laid* (bricks)
I *lie* (down)	I *lay* (down)	I have *lain* (down)
I *ring*	I *rang*	I have *rung*
I *rise*	I *rose*	I have *risen*
I *run*	I *ran*	I have *run*
I *seek*	I *sought*	I have *sought*
I *sing*	I *sang*	I have *sung*
I *steal*	I *stole*	I have *stolen*
I *swim*	I *swam*	I have *swum*
I *swing*	I *swung*	I have *swung*
I *write*	I *wrote*	I have *written*

3. TENSE SHIFTS

Changes in tense must occur for a good reason. In the following example, there is no justification for the shift:

SHIFT: I *ran* to his house and *tried* to find him, but I *arrive* too late. [Change *arrive* to *arrived*.]

REVISED: I ran to his house and tried to find him, but I *arrived* too late.

If it seems natural to you to use *arrive* rather than *arrived*, it may be that in your daily conversational habits you are not used to using, or even hearing, the past tense endings of verbs in standard English. If this is so, ask your instructor to recommend materials that will help you practice the standard tense forms.

NOTE: Do not drop the tense endings from past participles used as adjectives:

- The church boasted ornate, *stain* glass windows. [Change *stain* to *stained*.]

trans ——————— TRANSITIONS

Use a word or phrase to form a logical bridge, or *transition*, between two thoughts. The best transition to use is the one that most exactly expresses the logical relationship between two thoughts, sentences, or paragraphs.

Transitions are a special group of words and phrases that show how a piece of writing progresses logically from one idea to the next. Transitions connect parts of sentences, one sentence to another, and one paragraph to another. They express logical relations between ideas such as addition (*also, besides, furthermore*), contrast (*but, however, on the contrary*), result (*therefore, consequently*), and space or time (*beyond, in the distance, now, afterward*). The following passage uses transitions of time (in italics):

> *In its earliest stages,* war consisted solely of battle for hunting grounds. *Next* came struggles for pasture; *then* for tilled or tillable land.

There are many ways of showing the logical linkage between ideas; commonly used transitions follow:

TRANSITIONAL WORDS: accordingly, actually, afterward, again, also, and, before, beforehand, besides, but, consequently, eventually, finally, first, further, furthermore, gradually, hence, here, however, indeed, last, later, likewise, meanwhile, moreover, nevertheless, next, nonetheless, notwithstanding, nor, now, otherwise, second, similarly, soon, still, then, therefore, thereupon, this, too.

TRANSITIONAL PHRASES: after all, all in all, all things considered, and yet, as a result, at length, at the same time, by the same token, even so, for example, for the most part, for instance, for this purpose, generally speaking, in addition, in any event, in brief, in contrast, in fact, in like manner, in other words, in short, in spite of (that), in sum, in the first place, in the meantime, in the past, on the contrary, on the other hand, on the whole, to be sure, to sum up, to this end.

WEAK TRANSITION: She lost one fortune *and,* as if to spite fate, rapidly accumulated a second.
BETTER: She lost one fortune *but,* as if to spite fate, rapidly accumulated a second. [*But* more forcefully expresses the intended contrast.]

TRANSITION MISSING: I liked him. I thought his table manners needed improving. [The sudden contrast between these two thoughts is not smoothly bridged.]

BETTER: I liked him. *However,* I thought his table manners needed improving.

TRANSITION MISSING: On the whole, I think that educated people have made the best politicians. There are exceptions. [The second sentence follows too abruptly.]
BETTER: On the whole, I think that educated people have made the best politicians. *Of course,* there are exceptions.

Note the use of transitional words and phrases (italicized) in the following–somewhat shortened–paragraph by Schopenhauer:

What the address is to a letter, the title should be to a book; *in other words,* its main object should be to bring the book to those amongst the public who will take an interest in its contents. It should, *therefore,* be expressive. . . . The worst titles of all are those which have been stolen, *those, I mean,* which have already been borne by other books; for they are *in the first place* a plagiarism, and *secondly* the most convincing proof of a total lack of originality in the author. . . .

(For further information see **Coherence**, **Logic**, 5, and **Paragraph**.)

trite ———————— TRITENESS

Rewrite the marked passage to eliminate the triteness. Trite writing is dull, commonplace, and uninteresting. The fault may lie in the thought or the phrasing—and frequently in both. Use the following suggestions to eliminate triteness from your writing:

1. *Use livelier verbs.* Many common verbs do not make for specific, lively writing. Instead of writing, *"I had to eat* my sandwich quickly," write, "I *wolfed down* my sandwich." Which is more effective, "Boston *beat* New York 20 to 2," or "Boston *walloped* New York 20 to 2"?

2. *Use precise, vivid adjectives.* Many adjectives—*handsome, beautiful, nice, ugly*—are too vague to create a clear, specific picture in the reader's mind. You should communicate as precisely as possible the specific picture you have in mind. Instead of writing, "My father has a *handsome* face and *nice* eyes," write something like, "My father has a *weather-beaten, sportsman's* face with *gentle brown* eyes."

3. *Use effective figures of speech (comparisons).* Sometimes comparing one thing to another does the job better than a written explanation containing many words. Instead of writing, "We tried to get him to confess, but he *would not tell us a thing,"* write, "We tried to get him to confess, but he *was as uncooperative as a rhinoceros."*

CLICHÉS

A comparison that grows out of the situation you are writing about is likely to be fresh and appealing. A figure of speech that you have heard before is likely to be a cliché. Clichés are a special case of triteness. They are expressions that were once vivid and picturesque but are now so commonly used that they have lost their original force. Here are some examples of clichés (italicized):

- She was *as tight-lipped as a clam.*
- He wanted to live out in *the wide open spaces.*
- They made progress *by leaps and bounds.*
- On picnics one can relax and enjoy *Mother Nature.*
- I felt *as cool as a cucumber.*
- No one suspected the *trials and tribulations* they went through.
- Her cousin was *as quiet as a mouse.*

vague ———————— VAGUENESS

Rewrite the marked section in clear, direct, precise language. Vague writing is often described as *foggy* or *cloudy* because it lacks substance. It relies heavily on generalization and lacks specific, concrete ideas and facts. (See *Abstract Expressions, Diction,* and *Logic,* 2.)

There is nothing wrong with a clear, substantial generalization; for example, "Students who do not read well are unable to write well." You may not agree with this statement, but at least you have something specific to argue over. Compare that statement with this: "Students with problems in some areas have other problems as well." This statement is fuzzy, insubstantial, and evasive. It does not challenge the reader to think about a clear issue. It makes a noise without making a point.

Vague writing is like a picture out of focus. To develop a clear, precise writing style, focus your mind on the idea or image you want to present before you commit it to paper. If you see it clearly in your mind's eye, you have a good chance of bringing it out clearly on paper. Foggy writing mirrors foggy thinking:

> **VAGUE:** Professor Moss is a tough teacher whose personality turns me off.
> **CLEARER:** Professor Moss grades much too harshly and is insulting to students who challenge his ideas.

> **VAGUE:** I voted again for Mayor Dexter because her policies have helped the city improve in many ways, as we can see all around us.
> **CLEARER:** I voted again for Mayor Dexter because she has erased the city's budget deficit, built a new hospital and library, and helped improve relations between the police and the public.

VARIETY IN
SENTENCE PATTERNS ———— var

Develop a lively style by varying the *structures* and *lengths* of your sentences.

Good writers are always juggling a limited number of basic sentence patterns, balancing one against another to avoid monotony and to create a pleasing, rhythmic flow. You will find these basic structures easy to remember *because you know them already;* you already possess an array of skills that you are probably not aware you have. Substituting one pattern for another, we shall run a sample passage through a sequence of changes to show how virtually the same *ideas* can be expressed through a variety of *forms.*

1. STRUCTURAL VARIETY

Simple, Compound, and Complex Sentences

SAMPLE PASSAGE: We lost the first game. We vowed to even the score the next day out. [Here we have two *simple sentences*. Each simple sentence contains only one subject–verb nucleus—"We lost", "we vowed." The sentences stand uninterestingly next to each other. Notice how in the following examples the use of certain standard word structures creates meaningful relationships between these now separate ideas.]

USING COORDINATION: We lost the first game, *but* we vowed to even the score the next day out. [We now have a *compound sentence*, which is at least two simple sentences connected by a coordinating conjunction–*and, but, or, nor, for, yet,* or *so.* The connection by *but* ties these two separate thoughts into a relationship of contrast.]

USING A SUBORDINATE CLAUSE: *After we lost the first game,* we vowed to even the score the next day out. [A *subordinate clause* consists of a subordinating conjunction–like *after, because, since, when, although*–followed by, at the least, a subject and its verb–*we lost.* Try substituting *although* for *after.*]

USING A RELATIVE CLAUSE: After we lost the first game, we vowed *that we would even the score the next day out.* [A *relative clause* is a type of subordinate clause normally beginning with a relative pronoun such as *that, what, which, who,* or *whom.* Note: The combination of a main clause (simple sentence) with a subordinate clause results in a *complex sentence.* One of the ways to gain variety in sentence patterns is to create a pleasing alternation of *simple, compound,* and *complex* sentences.]

The following paragraph, from an essay by Robert Jay Lifton in *The Final Epidemic,* illustrates the skillful alternation of simple, compound, and complex sentences:

Although the idea of apocalypse has been with us throughout the ages, it has been within a religious context—the idea that God will punish and even eliminate man for his sins. [Complex] Now it is our own technology, and we are doing it ourselves. [Compound] Nor is it only the nuclear threat. [Simple] There are chemical warfare and germ warfare; destruction of the environment, the air we breathe or the ozone layer; and depletion of the world's resources, whether of energy or food. [Simple]

Different Types of Phrases

SAMPLE PASSAGE: We lost the first game. We vowed to even the score the next day out.

USING A PARTICIPIAL PHRASE: *Having lost the first game,* we vowed to even the score the next day out. [A *participial phrase* is a group of words beginning with a participle, the *-ing* form of a verb: in our example, *having*. It acts as an adjective and modifies the subject, *we*, of the main clause it introduces.]

USING A GERUND PHRASE: *Losing the first game* made us vow to even the score the next day out. [A *gerund phrase* looks like a participial phrase. It starts with a gerund, also the *-ing* form of a verb–in our example, *losing*–except that a gerund or whole gerund phrase acts as a noun. Here it acts as the subject of a sentence whose verb is *made*.]

USING A PREPOSITIONAL PHRASE: *After that first-game defeat,* we vowed to even the score the next day out. [A *prepositional phrase*, like *before work, inside the CIA,* or *after our defeat,* consists of a preposition followed by a noun–*defeat*–and any modifiers of that noun–*that first game*.]

USING AN INFINITIVE PHRASE: *To lose the first game* was such a blow that we vowed to even the score the next day out. [An *infinitive phrase* starts with an infinitive–in our example, *to lose*–which is followed by a noun, *game*, and any modifiers of that noun, *the first*. The infinitive phrase in this example acts as one whole noun, the subject of a sentence whose verb is *was*. Note that this sentence is also *complex*, consisting of a main clause beginning with *To lose* and a subordinate clause beginning with *that*.]

For more information on sentence patterns see **Subordination**. To learn how to knit sentences together to form a smooth paragraph, see **Transitions** and **Paragraph**.

Here is a brief paragraph, modified from J. E. Oliver's *Perspectives on Applied Physical Geography*, which achieves sentence variety by using subordination, coordination, and all of the phrase types we discussed:

> *Making use of loud noises* [gerund phrase] has been tried all over the world as a means *to change the weather.* [infinitive phrase] *In Europe, for example,* [prepositional phrases] people have tried *to prevent hailstorms,* [infinitive phrase] *for* [coordinating conjunction] hail has always caused considerable damage to vineyards. *To stop the hail from forming,* [infinitive phrase] farmers in northern Italy fired cannons at thunderclouds. Others felt *that they could stop storms* [relative clause] by *ringing church bells loudly.* [gerund phrase] Surprisingly, in some places *ringing bells* and *firing cannons* [gerund phrases] did seem to reduce the amount of crop damage by hail. This method became so popular *that it was finally outlawed.* [relative clause] Too many people were killed by *misfiring cannons* [prepositional phrase] and *by lightning* [prep. phr.] *striking bell towers* [participial phrase].

2. SENTENCE-LENGTH VARIETY

Good writers vary the pace and rhythm of their prose by mingling long, short, and medium-length sentences in any extended passage, as in the following paragraph (slightly modified from *Lunar Science: A Post-Apollo View*, by Stuart Ross Taylor):

> The *Apollo 11* landing on the moon took place on July 20, 1969, at 3:17:40 P.M., Eastern Standard Time, near the southern edge of Mare Tranquillitatis. [medium-length sentence] The site was named Tranquillity Base. [short] Astronauts Neil Armstrong and Edwin Aldrin collected 21.7 kilograms of samples in twenty minutes of hurried collecting toward the end of their two-hour sojourn (EVA, or extra-vehicular

activity) on the lunar surface. [medium to long] These samples were received in the quarantine facilities of the Lunar Receiving Laboratory in Houston on July 25. [short] Four weeks of intensive examination began. [short] A team of scientific workers (the Lunar Sample Preliminary Examination Team, or LSPET, comprising eleven NASA scientists and fifteen other scientists from universities and government agencies) carried out preliminary geologic, geochemical, and biological examination of the samples, providing basic data for the Lunar Sample Analysis Planning Team (LSAPT). [long] Many of the first-order conclusions about the samples (such as their chemical uniqueness, their great age, and the absence of water, organic matter, and life) were established in this period. [medium]

Note the sequence of sentence lengths in Taylor's paragraph: medium/short/medium–long/short/short/long/medium.

wdy ——————————— WORDINESS

Express your ideas in fewer words. Do not pad your sentences with unnecessary, repetitious phrasing. Avoid the unnecessary repetition of *words* and *ideas*:

WORDY: The novel *Don Quixote*, by Cervantes, is a novel that satirizes the dying age of chivalry. [Why repeat the word *novel*? A simple revision cuts out *four* needless words.]

BETTER: The novel *Don Quixote*, by Cervantes, satirizes the dying age of chivalry.

WORDY: *In my opinion, I personally believe* that our system of government is the best. [*In my opinion, personally,* and

I believe are three ways of phrasing the same *idea.* Do not use them all at once.]
BETTER: I believe that our system of government is best.

WORDY: *In the modern world of today,* the human race is enjoying the fruits of a long technological revolution *that took place throughout the entire period of the machine age.*
BETTER: Today the human race is enjoying the fruits of a long technological revolution. [All that has been left out is repetition that adds nothing.]

(See **Repetition.**)

Where possible, use short, direct grammatical constructions:

INDIRECT: Bill made the salad, and *the cake was baked by Henrietta.* [Use the active voice instead of the passive. See **Passive Voice.**]
DIRECT: Bill made the salad, and Henrietta baked the cake.

TOO LONG: I was responsible for overall maintenance, but *it was* Phil *who* did most of the repair jobs.
SHORTER: I was responsible for overall maintenance, but Phil did most of the repair jobs.

Some common wordy expressions to avoid:

WORDY	CONCISE
Along the line of	About
Crisis situation	Crisis
Due to the fact that (he objected)	Because (he objected)
Emergency situation	Emergency
For a long period of time	For a long time
For the purpose of	For
In spite of the fact that (he left)	Despite (his leaving)
In the event that	If

PROGRESS CHART

You will find the following columns useful for recording the errors you have made in your written assignments throughout the term. Use the first column to list the errors in your first composition, the second column for the errors in your second assignment, and so forth. For convenience, use the correction symbols only; next to each write how many times that particular error occurs in that composition: for example, FRAG (2). You should be able to see your progress—and your main problems—revealed more and more as the term goes on.   English ———.

ASGT. # DATE GRADE	ASGT. # DATE GRADE	ASGT. # DATE GRADE	ASGT. # DATE GRADE	ASGT. # DATE GRADE	ASGT. # DATE GRADE

PROGRESS CHART (*cont.*)

ASGT. # DATE GRADE	ASGT. # DATE GRADE	ASGT. # DATE GRADE	ASGT. # DATE GRADE	ASGT. # DATE GRADE	ASGT. # DATE GRADE

SPELLING PROGRESS CHART

List in the following columns the *correct* forms for the words you misspell on each composition. Your chart will develop into an excellent diagnosis of your spelling problems.

English _____.

ASGT. # DATE GRADE	ASGT. # DATE GRADE	ASGT. # DATE GRADE	ASGT. # DATE GRADE	ASGT. # DATE GRADE	ASGT. # DATE GRADE

SPELLING PROGRESS CHART (*cont.*)

ASGT. # DATE GRADE	ASGT. # DATE GRADE	ASGT. # DATE GRADE	ASGT. # DATE GRADE	ASGT. # DATE GRADE	ASGT. # DATE GRADE